DOES CHRISTIANITY KILL CULTURE?

ARTHUR CHINGWARU

WESTBOW
PRESS®
A DIVISION OF THOMAS NELSON
& ZONDERVAN

WestBow Press books may be ordered through booksellers or by contacting:

WestBow Press
A Division of Thomas Nelson & Zondervan
1663 Liberty Drive
Bloomington, IN 47403
www.westbowpress.com
844-714-3454

ISBN: 978-1-6642-2689-0 (sc)
ISBN: 978-1-6642-2691-3 (hc)
ISBN: 978-1-6642-2690-6 (e)

Library of Congress Control Number: 2021904848

Print information available on the last page.

WestBow Press rev. date: 05/03/2021

CONTENTS

INTRODUCTION

Through culture, we develop a sense of belonging, personal and cognitive growth, and the human intellectual achievement. Culture is a social behaviour and standard that exists in human society. Culture has always been mixed with Christianity. Without knowing where each begins and where each ends. We are unable to tell which role is taken by culture and which role Christianity takes in our lives.

Although Christ was born in a Jewish family, he would not be said to be of a Jewish culture but a Man of All cultures. He came to be a light to everybody in his or her different culture, his or her religion, or tradition. Christianity believes in looking after all creation.

This book will gradually explain to the reader what culture is, and then systematically explain to the reader Christianity so they know what Christianity is. After knowing the two separately, then how do the two work together. Has our knowledge of the two changed? Since we have known them, are they able to work together, how far they are going to work together. We have to reflect on the knowledge we had of them (culture and Christianity) before. What we knew of them before and what we now know are quite different.

Since these two things may affect our lives, (one of them or both), how are we going to take them? Do we have a choice of taking all of them, or take the one and leave the other. Since we now know them, that means we are making an informed choice of the two.

When we saw the topic, did we have our own answers, are they different from what we now know. If the answers we had before are different to what we now know, is this going to be our life application? This is going to affect us one way or the other, whichever way we choose, either culture or Christianity it is going to be our life application.

Since both of them have been explained fully it may help us to take an informed choice that may help us in future.

The reason why the author had to choose this topic is that it happened before and it is still happening to this present day. The way it affected them before should affect us differently today because we now know how it is affecting us after we are given how it affected each other before.

ACKNOWLEDGEMENTS

My grateful thanks go to my wife Rudo who would be alone by the time she was supposed to have my company. She was tolerant to allow me to carry on at odd hours. My greatest honour go to my children and their spouses: Anesu, Patience, John, Kingsley-T and Marilyn, they showed their greatest appreciation to see me writing. I am very much indebted to the following: Mr Thompson Mandaza who assisted to formulate the very first paragraphs and the structure of the book: I very much appreciate the assistance I got from

Mr Shepherd Kucherera, Mr Dydmus Muchineuta, Mr Ranga Chivasa snr. My grateful thanks to my pastor Rev. Ken Marange, who was shepherding me during the time of writing. The pastor of my family Rev. Christopher Chikoore who also assisted in formulating some of the passages. There are some who were not mentioned by name but their assistance made it to be how it is.

My greatest indebtedness goes to my fellow congregants who gave me the encouragement which gave me the zeal. All my grandchildren who made their contribution in a funny way.

INSPIRATION

I was inspired to write by Luke, the one who wrote the gospel of "Luke and the Acts of the Apostles". We are told that Luke was a physician, but had decided to leave a heritage for us as to what we are reading today.

I said to myself, if someone 2000 years ago, decided to leave a heritage, which is helping us today. What are we leaving for the next generation?

I said to myself, with the grace of the Lord I will do something for that generation, that made me to start writing.

What made me to choose the topic (Does Christianity Kill Culture?) was Acts chapter 19 when Paul had arrived in Ephesus and found that they were worshiping their goddess Diana. Paul preached that there was a living God. Business for those who were making shines for Diana started going down, so those who made a living out of making shrines, started telling people that Christianity was killing their culture.

Currently when discussing matters with fellow congregants, it appears that belief still exists, that is where the need for researching on this arose.

Arthur Chingwaru: (cowsheepscapegoat@yahoo.co.uk).

27.02.2018 DOES CHRISTIANITY KILL CULTURE. ACTS CHAPTER 19:

The motive of this book is to enlighten to its reader on the relationship that exists between culture and Christianity, and how culture exists, and how Christianity exists.

Here culture has to be taken in a broader sense: accordingly, all the different cultures have been taken as a single entity: some cultures have been singled out for special mention, but not all cultures have been accommodated.

CHAPTER 1

CULTURE:

According to the: (Concise Oxford English Dictionary): Culture is the way people conduct themselves towards others. Some behaviours and things that are joined in such a way that they do not separate, ideas or theory containing various conceptual elements, and influenced understanding that are learned through a process of association. This type of learning may result in what may be called associative learning; any learning process may become associated with a particular.

It distinguishes members of a certain group from the other; it surrounds and has or holds within it, language, religion and social habits, all are embodied in culture. Sometimes culture may be faced with a dilemma that most cultural may not have written down guidelines, as a result everyone tend to put it their own way they might find suitable to them but not suitable to the whole society. So, anyone who might want to follow might find themselves groping their way into it. It may be found that one cultural aspect might be implemented differently depending on how influential the one who is introducing it. Some of the cultural aspects may be bent to or to please someone who is involved disregarding what it really should be. Culture may also be determined by where people live, by their gender, language, customs laws, dress, architectural style, social standards and religion. What people hold to be true in that particular group and their beliefs, all these will determine their values.

(Tali Sharot) The belief shapes people's minds towards certain things, which now shape their lifestyles. Sometimes these things will make people to be bound together, doing it unconsciously. A social habit is something that is ingrained in you in such a way that you will be doing it automatically without thinking. These could be negative or positive habits. Social habits influence our behaviour and determine our actions. These social habits are transmitted to the next generation it means that; it is a secret history of our ancestors. That is why these behaviours will always follow one another without any command from anyone. This history is of their habits is encoded in the DNA. (*Deoxyribonucleic acid*: is a carrier of genetic information)

(The Guardian 27 August 2017: Tali Sharot: Life Styles) The way we exist every day, such as the way we share our day-to-day life as people in a place or time is culture. A set of shared attitudes, values goals and practices that makes an institution or organisation focused on making their culture stand and not shaken, always transmitted to the next generation.

(Khan Academy :) (Christianity in the Roman Empire) In those early days, Christians were openly persecuted, but now it is no longer being open, (although we still have a few examples like the Hindus who are still persecuting Christians openly) there is an unrevealed persecution of believers currently, worldwide, because there is tension between culture and Christianity. This persecution was inherited from the apostles who were the first ones to suffer this persecution. The aim of this book is trying to reveal some minute differences that might exist, such as what exists between families, when one family member decides to follow Christianity and the other members of the same family decide to follow cultural activities, the relationship becomes strained in such a way that their relationship might be torn to pieces. We are hoping to see how this hidden hatred might be revealed and see how it could be eliminated, and accommodate each other.

(https//explorable.com/culture-and-personality) Culture refers to shared values, beliefs and norms of a specific group of people. Culture therefore influences the manner we learn, live and behave. Because of this, many theorists believe that culture is an important shaper of our personality, because it influences the way we learn, live and behave. The effect of culture to personality culture greatly contributes to the development of our beliefs and values, is that people who are born and bred in the same culture share common personality traits. There is a strong relationship between culture and personality, in addition, differences also influence the personality traits a person possesses. The study of culture has to go deeper, because the same culture when in primitive people compared to civilised people seem to differ, why? In addition, culture differs according to gender.

IF CULTURAL MAYBE CORRUPTED BY SIN IF IT IS OUTSIDE OF THE CHURCH:

As culture and Christianity exist contemporarily, they will always compromise to accommodate and complement the other. Sometimes Christians take things that are not Christian and trying to fill them with Christian meaning. By doing so, sometimes Christians are found to be living double standards, which may result in the end Christianity being diluted and becoming less and less a spiritually filled Christianity. Throughout history, all Christians have lived in specific cultural contexts, which they sometime take some and reject others. Depending on the nature of the cultural aspect, Christians may have a negative or positive response. Sometimes Christians take a more guarded approach to the cultures that surround them, that will mean they will take it with caution. Examples of the things that are taken with caution by Christians are like; alcohol, polygamy, divorce abortion, and some other such issues. This is where multiculturalism is at loggerheads with Christianity, because this is where some cultures are saying it is their rights regardless of what God says about it. Some Christians might reject a certain practice, while some cultures gladly accept it. Some cultures take honouring their ancestor seriously while some say it is unholy. The research goes on of trying to accommodate each other as Christians, but at the same time trying to find common ground, in order to be able to live together as Christians in a multicultural society of Christianity.

Sometimes cultural expressions have to be augmented and perfected by Christian revelation and the work of the church, because Christ is supreme to everything, he said, on you I will build my church, which means He is always looking at the church; He wants it to be treated with its Holiness. Culture is good but sometimes tainted by sin, and therefore, there is need for Christ to cleanse it. There is always tension between Culture and Christianity because sometimes Christianity may be defined in black and white, while culture has some grey areas, what can make Culture and Christianity work together? Because Christians came from different cultures, something is needed to harmonise them, that would mean looking at them closely and see which aspects need be left out. How can culture and Christianity be transformed for the glory of God? Both these two have to be transformed to the glory of God. If there is one aspect of the other that is tainted, it should not be taken aboard because it may corrupt the whole relationship that might exist between culture and Christianity. That is the reason why some aspects of culture are left out, it is not that the whole culture is killed, but only to straighten it and get it on board.

THE RELATIONSHIP BETWEEN CULTURE AND CHRISTIANITY ON LIBERALISM AND PROTECTIONISM:

(Machen J G) (Christianity and culture) Anyone is allowed to take their liberal views on culture not bound by the norms of culture. Society that stresses the freedom of individuals regardless of what that culture does. Protectionism in culture is that some governments even try protecting their culture, (they are those who may be trying to protect their culture from being absorbed by some foreign habit bringing them into their culture; this may be done by the government or some culturalism himself or herself. Culture is so wide that it cannot be said that it can be killed or not killed. It has so many aspects, which might need a thorough examination in order to come up with a solution. It could be called a strong part of the people's lives; it influences their views, and values, beliefs and norms of a specific group of people. Culture therefore, influences the manner we learn, live and behave. Because of this, many theorists believe that culture is an important shaper of our personality, Values our humour and there are some important cultural aspects on the way humour is used, their hopes, their loyalties, their worries and fears. When working with people and building relationships with them, it helps to have some perspective and understanding of their cultures. Culture helps to identify the similarities and differences in people.

(Cliff's Notes.com) In basic sociological terms, culture can be defined as the language, norms, values, beliefs, and more of them together form the people's way of life. It is a combination of elements that affect how people think, how they act, and what they own. Every nation has a culture, but not every nation is Christian in culture.

A CULTURAL MIND SET IS SOMETIMES VERSUS CHRISTIANITY:

Christianity began in the first century AD as a Jewish sect in Judea, after Jesus died, but quickly spread throughout the Roman Empire. As if there was no persecution Christianity quickly became the official religion. Attack on Christianity and Churches are increasing these days in our society. A secular mind set is manifesting in some form. There are some who pretended to be Christians but gained little knowledge, are the ones who have turned back and start to scorn the church and are critiques of the church. (Ashford/Views on Relationship between Christianity and Culture) Revelations 3:11 There are so many forces that are fighting against Christianity, but it is for the Christian to wear the amour of faith and deal with them faithfully but boldly. The Saviour came down to set an example of how to deal with such forces. To put on the amour of faith is not only to attend church services, but to be spiritually filled. We learn that when Jesus was baptised the Holy Spirit came down and rested on him. When he went to the wilderness, he was spiritually filled; that is, to be full of joy coming from the love of God: When Jesus was in the wilderness, He was spiritually filled, as a result he was able to resist any temptations. It is for us to always ask the Lord to fill us with this Holy Spirit, because without that Holy Spirit, we are not going to be able to resist the temptation. Jesus put an emphasis on putting on the amour of the Holy Spirit when he spoke to Nicodimus. (John 3:5). We have to repent and examine our hearts each time we repent so that we are not tempted again, because each time we are fighting a spiritual warfare.

We are fighting a war that started in heaven a long time ago when started misbehaving in heaven. The devil wants it to appear like this war will never be won, like that day on the cross, when it appeared like the devil had won, but came the resurrection day, that is when the victory was for us all. Our Saviour came down to earth to set an example and to show that it is not an easy war but that it can be won, once we put on the spiritual amour of faith and hope, and carry our cross like He did. Christ himself fought that war and won without weapons of war like guns, but spiritual guns, let us carry those Spiritual guns. Other than the fact that Christianity fought the primitive of the people and brought civilisation, Christianity is still playing a very pivotal role in shaping people's lives. What Christianity is doing is to unify families that could be torn apart. Although multi-culturalism is trying to do away with Christianity, Christianity is there to unify nations that could be taking each other as enemies. Even if Christianity and governments did not come together to formulate one thing, there is a coordination somewhere. When governments want to discipline people in a harsh way, Christianity does it gently without hardening the lives of the people. People find themselves discipline that even the governments will appreciate it that half their work has been accomplished by Christianity. The influence of Christianity to people's lives is very essential and enormous, that otherwise nations would be enemies to each other.

CULTURE HAS GOT SOME INFLUENCE ON THE VIEWS OF THE PEOPLE:

(Psychological Science.org) Since culture is shared among a group of people, each member has to conform to the way the people in that group behave. Each member has to fit in or risk being a misfit or falling into the category of being an outcast. Sometimes they do not have to learn it, or like it, it is in their DNA. Culture shapes people's personalities, people who are born and bred in the same culture share common personalities and distinguishing qualities of a person. The way culture affects our thinking depends on the way we see the world, if we see the world differently, it will influence us differently too. The other factor that influences culture is that people are born in that culture and grew in that culture; so their thinking is influenced by that culture. If for example, people have studied many cultures they will think differently than those who have grown in one culture. Culture influences every aspect of the life of the people whether they like it or not, because it is inborn.

Beliefs and causes of diseases are influenced by culture; some disease is influenced by the beliefs in the culture the way people will seek help will also be influenced by culture. The influence of culture in our health is a big one if mum and dad had different cultures originally; children will struggle because they are caught in between and will struggle on which culture to follow. Degrees of pain are also influenced by culture, some members of culture have some degree of tolerance. Members of a group can influence how they seek medical help, as an example, (age or gender) plays a very influential role in determining what culture they belong to. Culture is an important shaper of our personalities just doing it without thinking: "inborn."

THE EFFECT OF THE JEWISH CULTURE TO CHRISTIANITY:

It is interesting to note that Christianity developed from the Jewish culture, while the Jews were under Roman rule, which means sometime the Jews were compelled to follow some of the Roman culture. That is where Christianity emerged as a world religion, there must be some divine powers connected to that. (Jews for Jesus .org) Early Christianity had so many difficulties, Jesus was a Jew and all his twelve disciples were Jews, Christianity did not start during Jesus' mission on earth, but immediately after He had left. Before He left, He promised that you will receive power, but He ordered them not to leave Jerusalem before they had received this power. What happened at Pentecost (Acts Chapter 2) (KJV), as promised by Jesus that He would not leave us comfortless, and that when He comes He would dwell in us forever. To imagine that these people who were of Jewish culture were the ones to start the Christian movement after Jesus had left them was not easy. That means Jews were having so many sects, Christianity added to the many they had. Their task was to convince the people that it was not meant to kill their culture. The first task was to convince the people so they could understand that

Jesus was the (promised) Messiah they were waiting for (as is happening currently some are still doubting whether Jesus is the real one), and that He was the anointed one and that He was divine as well as human and that to follow His movement was to follow something divine, so those who would quickly accept that He was a Messiah would still have some reservations, or some would have some neutralised faith. Some of this can still be noticed in our life application today, it is still difficult to have deep faith and start worshiping Him in truth and in spirit, yet that is what it means to be called a Christian as mentioned by Jesus when He spoke to the Samaritan woman in John 4:24. Also the task that was faced by the early Christian was to try to convince the Jews that Christianity was for all. We are still asking for the Holy Spirit to guide us because there are still many out there who still need to know Him.

THE ATTITUDE OF THE JEWS TO THE EARLY CHURCH WAS ANTE-GOD:

(Davies P.E 1945 just.org.) : These people were practising Judaism before Christ came, even though He did not dismantle Judaism, but some people saw some truth in Christianity Christ did not start that movement, but only that it gained momentum on its own as many people followed this movement. Attitude of Jews to the Early Church was anti-God) during the time of Nero the Jews put the blame on the Christians for fire that had happened in Jerusalem. Christians faced hatred from two fronts, from Nero and from the Jews, because the Jews were saying why are you promoting the one we condemned and crucified. So they were adding fuel to the anger of Nero. There were anti-Christian riots in most of the provinces of Asia Minor. Because of what was done to Christians by the Jews in those days made some Christians to be sceptical of the Jews. But the world council of churches is saying Christians should not seek revenge. We get our example from Jesus who, when it was very painful on the cross, said Father forgives them for they know not what they do. Christians should always follow His example. What people should realise is that God knows that all the people on earth are His and He loves them all no Gentile or Jew all the people are His. It is up to the people to take each other as brothers because we are children of the same Father.

CULTURE MAY CHANGE AS IT EVOLVES FROM ONE GENERATION TO THE OTHER:

(Mouden C. EL/onlinelibrary. Wiley.com) Culture is transmitted from generation to generation by means of simulation (that is, coping from the one that was there before you). If there are no longer suitable behaviours, they are removed as the culture evolves, as the population changes and the rapidly changing environments. These changes occur in order to facilitate the more suitable ones and the more appropriate. This may prove that there are so many factors that make culture to change. The changes may be in three forms: vertical; (that is, changing from big to small), oblique, (that is, when it changes in generations rather than centuries); and horizontal, (that is, when the change is organisational) transmission the other causes of many changes is that, while culture is transmitted by learning from others, the learner might not copy everything from their teacher; the learner might also add some variables, the other most common factor is that this transmission from generation to generation is done only through verbal communication. This kind of transmission (verbal) in this kind of transmission some aspects may be lost or some might be added. However, some aspects may be lost as it is relayed from generation to generation, and as it passes from one generation to another? The parents of each generation teach their children and they learn how to do it the people before them did it. Something might change sometime, other people could affect other beliefs, which might mean culture can be modified overtime, as time changes, and it passes through learning and teaching repeatedly.

AS THE ISRAELITES' CULTURE DEVIATED FROM THE AGREEMENT, THEY GOT SOME PUNISHMENT FROM GOD:

(Bibletools.org RTD CGG) (Forerunner commentary) They forgot what the Lord had done for them, yet they had promised to abide by their agreement. They were now relying on their own, and forgetting the covenant they had made with God. That tends to be a human weakness, of forgetting so easily. If we can remember how much they had cried in their bondage in Egypt, they would vow to keep the covenant, but within a very short period they had forgotten all about it. God requires our faithfulness, even currently; let us not forget that we are making a covenant with Him which we must try to keep at any cost, this helps to keep our good relationship with Him. The covenant was not harsh with people, but it was only meant to have a closer relationship with, and to differentiate the chosen people from all other nations. As they had breached the covenant, God could not let them go without a punishment. The Israelites had forgotten that God had brought them out of bondage in Egypt, and they started worshiping other gods, which angered their God. They were delivered into the hands of their enemies, and most of them were exiled in a foreign land, who forced them to adopt their culture, to deviate from God brings serious consequences. As they had sinned against the Lord, He put them out of His sight. The only solution when we have sinned is to turn back to Him and confess or we perish.

FROM TIME TO TIME CULTURE MAY SOMETIMES DEVIATE FROM GOD:

The problem arises when our culture values conflict with God's will for us. Let us not just take these things at face value, let us know that cultures have values that may deviate from God's Spiritual laws and truth. The problem that is faced by Christians is that, culture is passed on from generation to generation. Maybe those older generations did not know Christianity that is why some of what they did was antichrist. We cannot be asked to follow blindly when know well that some of them are antichrist, that is why we are asked to find a way of accommodating culture without causing any harm to our Christian relationship. (Christianity Today.com/how) As we walk in our Christian life, it is better to be on the alert and be watchful to those things that would make us drift from near our Father. Some of the things are so hidden that we might not notice them as being sins. If we are not watchful, by the time we will realise, we will have drifted far away that sometimes to return will start to be impossible. Ephesians 5:16, is reminding us that Satan plays his cards wisely, if for example in football match your opponent is tactful,, and you are not tactful, you will be out witted. The devil's tactic might be in wealth, if that would make us busy as to have not even a short time for your spiritual welfare. We all want wealth because it is good for us, but let us always take stock to see if things are still balancing. Do you still have time for your spiritual welfare? If you still have time, congratulations. Worldly things such as entertainments, are they giving you time on your schedule of entertainments? Eternal life must begin inside our hearts, are we not entertained with worldly things so as to be left without eternal entertainment. I would not ask you to abandon them, but only ask you to reflect on them and compare with the reflection of your church life. Are they still balancing? Check that with 1 John 2:15-16 and make a u turn if that has p The Similarities in Culture and Christianity explained further:

(According to David Wittenberg), there is no such a question, culture is a generic term meaning for what people believe in and do. There is no similarity; they belong to two different classes. The question could be what is the influence of Christianity to a certain particular culture? (DR. Bruce Ashford) seems to agree with Wittenberg, because he also sees culture and Christianity as opposing factors. But according to lay people, they see it like those who may be practising Christianity are the ones who have their own culture, that is why they were asking to have them defined, so that each and every one stands alone. They want them defined so as for them to know He sees politics and culture standing on one side; and he sees like Christianity giving in. Bruce points at multiculturalism as an example, where multiculturalism is dominant to Christianity.

(Christian Re-think), tries to find out whether Christianity is a religion or not? They see churches failing to represent true Christians; they may be taking it from Jesus' conversation with the Samaritan woman, where Jesus is very emphatic that he, who worships Him, must worship Him in truth and in Spirit. This is to say that Christians must really mean what they do. They say the onus is on us to follow how Jesus has already shown His love to man by sacrificing His blood for us. According to them, it is us who must establish the heavenly kingdom here on earth; other than looking forward for the heavenly kingdom to come as a miracle. Pointed out exactly what you do.

CHAPTER 2

THERE ARE SOME CONSEQUENCES IF WE EMBARK ON UNHOLY PRACTICES:

(Institute of basic Life Principles) The major thing that causes to sin is lust or mare greed or some wickedness in us. These things combine to make us sin. When Jesus was praying in Gethsemane, when He came back they were asleep, but He woke them up saying Keep watch so that you are not tempted. . This means that temptations are around us all the time we have to keep watch all the time, because temptations have no boundaries. What we are all striving for, is to come out victorious after those temptations. If anything, let the battle be fought in our thoughts because that is the manufacturing factory. The first thing to pray for is our thoughts, even when Jesus was tempted; it was thought that the devil came to. Once the devil conquers your brain, he has won his battle. You are made to believe that you are the only one with this problem, and you are made to ask why me? Yet you are not the only one it is only your brain that is in captivity. (openbible.infor/ (1 Corinthians 6:9: Jude 1:7) (KJV) Impure thinking causes us to have impure habits, which is a clear way of separation from God. God is pure; He wants us to be pure so we can have good relationship with Him. We are fighting a battle with the devil who is always trying to separate us from God our Father. Satan brings falsehood in our minds for us to always think that we are already defeated. Always temptations are around us some of the temptations do not appear to be temptations at all, but to find ourselves involved in them and sometimes unable to come out of them. Christ came to be an example, and to make us know that temptations can be overcome.

WE SHOULD NOT CONTINUE TO SIN JUST BECAUSE GOD IS MERCIFUL:

(Biblehub.com/(romans 6:15/romans 6:1) God's grace is free, God's grace is sometimes prevenient, and that has misled us because we are tempted to think that after all it will still come because it is prevenient. Yet He is the one who says there is time for everything, time for grace and time for judgement, do we agree to that? This book is pleading with the reader to take advantage of the grace period to receive the grace while it still time for grace. Let us not be tempted to keep on sinning just because there is grace. God has set us free from the law; this does not mean that we should go on sinning? It is not like that, the time for judgement is definitely coming. We must be found prepared. God Himself does not like sin that is the reason why His son had to die on the cross to save us from sin; therefore, we cannot go on sinning. Romans 6:1 Paul states clearly that we should not go on sinning just because we will have mercy. When we leave our sinful ways we must not look back. God is merciful when we do not know, but when we are doing it on purpose just because He is merciful, there is time for everything. When we were baptised that means we have left our old ways and clinging on to the lord who is blameless. Then why should we go back to our old ways. When Jesus was resurrected, He never went back to the grave. When we left our old ways means that we were resurrected with Jesus, why then should we go back to our old ways yet Jesus never went back.

CORRUPTION AND SIN GO HAND IN HAND:

"Corruption is worse than any sin because it hardens the heart against feeling shame or guilt or feeling God's call for conversion" Those words were said by Pop Francis (Vatican City). (Rose Ackerman/corruption Causes and Consequences) Corruption has many different shapes and has got very serious consequences. It has damaging effects on the economy and on society. It will make us drift away from our creator who is pure. He is pure, so corrupt things do not want to stay near Him. So if you are following corrupt ways, it is you who is distancing yourself from Him. Corruption is an abuse of trusted position. This mean if you accept a bribe, you will be twisting the case against the innocent in favour of the guilty. This is found to happen mostly to developing nations and this has hindered the progress greatly and has held back their growth greatly. This has dragged for quite some time, without solution in sight. We plead with those countries which are developed to come to the rescue, because as a result it is causing death and suffering to innocent souls. It appears like it is a problem affecting those developing countries, but in the long run it is everyone's problem. When souls perish that were not supposed to perish, it becomes everyone's problem. The bad thing with corruption is that it affects those who claim to be pure Christians, because it comes like something very normal and sometimes it does not appear like a bribe. That is the reason why we must ask for divine intervention because of its nature and how it comes to us.

CULTURE MAY NOT BE FREE FROM SIN:

(Ransomed Heart.com/sin) Our calling as Jesus' disciples is to live a victorious life, a life where we live and reign over sin. Freedom from sin is possible in this life, when we shun and live a Christ like life. Romans 5:17, although sin had entered us through one man, there is also one man who brought a new covenant and His sacrificial blood brought us salvation. By following those simple steps which were given as an example by Jesus Himself, we are promised eternal life, a promise to those who live like Christ, can triumph over sin's power and over death's threat through the power and protection of Jesus. Originally we were destined for death, but through the grace of Jesus Christ we are ransomed and redeemed.

Jesus wants us to be conformed to his image; everyone who beholds the glory is transformed into that image. (2 Corinthians 3:18) (KJV), if anything, we have to reflect Christ's life, because that is the purpose for which He came. Jesus teaches us that there is victory over sin if we follow his example, the example is simple and straight forward, and Jesus conquered sin. If we live a life free from sin, we can be like him. If we live such a life, we will be pillars of God's temple. There is no condemnation to those who do His will and take His image. The glory that the Spirit imparts on us, makes us Holy, it is excellent and lasts longer than the glory that Moses experienced. Beholding the nature of God with unveiled minds, we can be more like him.

If we would compare the present and the past, it will be seen that morally the standards are lower than they were; we are hiding behind rights. Whenever we want to change these standards, we hide behind saying it is their rights. Look around you, what was law before is now the norm. People have inherited the sins of their fore fathers they have inherited that culture so they have also inherited everything that comes with that culture. Sin tries to distort the way we understand scriptures, so it is up to every Christin to try break away from those forces, which will be working against us, God, expects us to come clean to Him without any blemishes. Sometimes culture is interwoven in us in such a way that we have to be very vigilant so as to be able to follow what the Bible requires us to do to be pure Christians.

USUALLY, THE PEOPLE'S LOYALTY IS VESTED IN THEIR CULTURE:

The law to their culture does not bind people always but they are bound by loyalty. In normal circumstances people tend to be very loyal to their culture in such a way that they do not need any laws to tell them to obey their culture but only their loyalty. Families are bound together by being loyal to that which brings them together. You will find that if there is no loyalty that family will appear to be a divided family. When you are loyal, that means you are very devoted and faithful to whatever you are for, whether it be a family, a nation, or an individual, if there is loyalty that means there is a very closer tie that will make a very strong bond. That is the reason why sometimes culture appears to be very strong because people are connected to cultures by loyalty, instead of by law. Law sometimes forces people to obey it whether you are loyal or not, so people will obey it to those limits, whereas with loyalty, it will always be free will.

AS SOCIETY CHANGES FROM ONE GENERATION TO THE OTHER, SO CULTURE DOES ALSO CHANGE SLIGHTLY:

(Frederic E. Abbe Professor of Economics/Evolution of Culture) Sometimes culture is determined by environmental instability. That is to say, culture might be determined by the situation that is available at that moment. There are times when culture may resist the environmental changes but in most cases it bows to the environment. When things are stable, culture seem to relax unlike when things go tough the culturalism will want to tighten and want to appease those spirits which are responsible for culture. Generations and cultures both change as time changes, culture evolves slowly, and due to environmental changes, technological advances, economies and interactions. Regardless of all those changes, the underlying values remain fairly static.

Culture is made up of customs, attitudes and beliefs that are unique to each group of people. New philosophical ideas and technological advances can lead to cultural change. Cultural change can also occur through diffusion, which means there are so many changes as they change from one generation to the other, and as the nations are becoming more and more multicultural.

Sometimes some bad things are committed in the name of Christianity, such as wars that are happening, lives are lost some atrocities are committed. Sometimes these things are made in the name of Christianity and Christianity tends to be blamed. These may be caused through men greedy, man is power hungry, and human nature seeks its own ways rather than God's ways. Some of these things have caused a distortion of Christianity. True Christianity should be joined to Jesus Christ in whom we have faith because of what He did for us on the cross, and is still living among us through His Holy Spirit. God uses the church in His plan to rescue the people, but sometimes we Christians are full of unbelief, unbelief is the enemy of God, because that unbelief will lead you to do things that are very unpleasing to God.

THE RELATIONSHIP BETWEEN CHRISTIANITY AND CULTURE IS A VOLATILE ONE:

(Bruce and Ashford) A Christian is a man of all cultures, Christianity might borrow some culture, but might not want to take them as they are, but to modify them slightly, this will mean that culture may still recognise them as their norm while Christianity has taken them on board. Similarly, culture might take some aspects from Christianity and comfortably accommodate them as theirs. Some religions in some cultures believe that there is God as do the Christians, although in some religions they will differ in their approach, for example, some Buddhists can practise Buddhist principles while at the same time practising Christianity. Buddhists are so liberal on that they do not have to tell you that you have to believe in anything. There is a very thin relationship between culture and religion. It appears religion is standing for the people because it says the people belong to God. There are times when culture shows it true colours, when it is required to express itself. The religion seems to understand the world and its people better than culture. Culture and religion go hand in hand. It is generally, (not as a rule) that if you are of a certain religion you will be of a culture that is practised with that religion. As they are so interwoven, you cannot separate them.

CULTURE AND CHRISTIANITY ARE EXISTING CONTEMPORARILY:

(Leaderu.com.orgs/probe/docs/ Christianity and Culture) There is a misconception that Christianity is destroying culture, but do we sometimes examine our deeds if they are not anti-God? If there is a practice that is common to Christianity it becomes a Christian culture. Since Christianity derives its name from Christ, Jesus Christ was a Jew; this does not necessarily mean that it is a Jewish culture because as soon as Jesus left, Christianity spread rapidly to other nations, taking their cultures. So it becomes difficult to align it to a single particular culture. We live with culture, stay with culture, we communicate with culture: pass it on to the next generation through words and gestures and actions. It expresses and communicates our identity and the identity of the people we interact with. We have to accept that it is not everything that is bad in culture. There are some good aspects in culture. For those aspects, which are not good, we have to consult the scriptures. The scriptures will reveal to us what directions we have to follow. Christian values are so good to some people that they like to follow Christianity without going deeper into it. Otherwise, family background or what happened to them in their lives might compel them to do that. What happened in their lives before or the environment in which they grew up might have a bearing in what we see on them.

CHRIST DOES NOT LOOK AT CULTURE THE WAY WE DO LOOK AT IT:

The role of Christianity in civilisation has always been intertwined with the history and formation of western society. Christianity did not force widows.... During the middle ages churches have replaced the Roman Empire as a unifying force; the cultural influence of churches is big. So what Christianity has done to society has helped to strength the relationship that exists between culture and Christianity. Although politicians have high jacked it and called it human rights, yet Christianity started without sounding trumpets. The up lifting of people's welfare by Christianity is not only historical but also for current and future. Churches set up schools and universities, which are still existing to this date and giving people the civilisation required for the alleviation of human suffering (Gotquestion. org/Cultural Christian) There, are so many Christians who believe in both of the two, as long as they are called Christians they are fine, they are not worried about being spiritually filled. "God is a spirit: and they that worship Him must worship Him in spirit and in truth "God is present everywhere and all the time. The best thing in worship is to ask the Holly

Spirit to guide us so as to worship Him in spirit and in truth. The Holy Spirit prays for us. Let us ask to be divinely possessed and for us to be so we perform spiritually whatever we do. These believers are nominal believers, they are socially following the two not specialising in any of the two, they reject the spiritual aspect which requires them to be biblically defined Christians, so Christianity is just a label. In some free nations, the gospel is presented as a costless addition to their lives; church going is one of their hobbies. In this way, these people are just accepting Jesus as one of the prophets. There is no surrendering one's self to the Lordship of Jesus, they are cultural Christians, do we really take Christ as the true-vine, and we as branches attached to the true-vine? (John 15:1-8) (KJV).Let us take a look at the apostles immediately after the Pentecost, did we have such thing as cultural Christianity? Refer to (Acts 11:26) (KJV). A believer must be exemplary and show strong faith in Christ in order for new Christians to know who Christ is. It appears today's Christians fear persecution; hence, keeping a lukewarm profile, cultural Christianity is not true Christianity.

Christianity has always been a cross culture, religion from its inception. No single dominant culture from where Christianity originated. Since then Christianity has taken its culture from so many different cultures, which makes it difficult to adopt a single culture.

Some people are left wondering what is happening that the Christian culture is dominant even to those who are not Christians will find themselves involved in the Christian culture. They find themselves involved in the Christian calendar, or Christian festive seasons like Christmas and New Year or Easter, they are all celebrated by none Christians. The parable of the Good Samaritan blends very well with human rights activists who claim that all human are equal regardless of race or colour. Feminist activists argue that sometimes women are looked down upon in the pulpit, yet the Samaritan woman preached and the whole city was converted. Mary was the first to see the risen Christ, and preached that Jesus said we me meet in Galilee, and they complied and met Him in Galilee.

CHRISTIANITY AND CULTURE; APPEAR TO HAVE SOMETHING IN COMMON:

What Christianity and culture have in common is that as the people get civilised they tend to lean to Christianity but Christianity did not say abolish your culture the cultures seem to modify some of the cultural habits without abandoning them so when Christianity accept that then those will be the things they will have in common. In fact modern culture is elevated from the old culture which was a bit primitive as its people join Christianity they take the civilisation in Christianity. That is to say, the people who were cultural are the ones who are today's Christians with their modified culture. This is not one sided, because as they come with their modified cultures, this has tended to neutralise some of the Christians who were originally not very strong Christians. Being influenced by Christianity some have come in with their unmodified cultures and tended to contaminate Christianity. So there is a danger to every side being dragged to the other side. That is when it becomes a sensitive issue.

Culture is human it is our day to day life, yet Christianity is formed from these people. This means there is not much difference if any, but faith is what they have in common, but it only differs, they are faithful in what? It is what they are faithful in, is what they are trying to join together.

WE CAN HAVE A PERFECT CULTURE IF WE FOLLOW WHAT CHRIST WANTS US TO DO:

(Paul Capan: Bible Answer man: We have very good examples of what culture is "Jesus shaped Culture". What some cultures accepted as the norms is what Christianity tries to discourage, such as forced sexuality, cultures tolerated as a norm but Christianity says there must be a choice on the other party so as to do it in agreement. Such things damaged culture. That is why Christianity is shaping all these things. (Institute of Faith, work and Economics) Since culture is our way of living, that means there is no hard and fast rule, only to say that as Christ came to set an example on earth, we are trying to emulate Him. That means that we are not dumping those ways, but only that since we are emulating Christ, we are just correcting our way of doing things. That means that as we shape ourselves, we will keep on reflecting on our deeds and behaviours will leave us closer to Him than we were before. That is the aim of this life that in the end we do find ourselves closer than to find ourselves being distanced from Him. What we are striving for is personal transformation; it is known very well that will mean taking a better shape. That is, we will have taken His shape both in deeds, truth and in spirit. We must definitely ask for His Spirit "that we were promised" for us to be changed inside out, that is to start from within us to then be seen by our deeds. What we are asking for is not only personal transformation, but that when we are changed we will also be able to make the world what pleases the Lord, that was His mission here on earth, was to transform it from where it was in bad shape, but leave it in good shape. Since we are following Christ's example, our deeds must be imitated by society that surrounds us. Whether it is culturalism or Christianity, the world has to be a good place to live in that will have happened through our good works. As Christianity spread, that is how civilisation spread, civilisation has helped quite a lot in shaping culture. Christianity started after Jesus was accused, prosecuted, and condemned to death some two thousand years ago. Compared to other histories, His movement is the only one that has survived for over 2 000 years that means there is something that must be looked at closely. This must be put into research to try to find out what is in that, because other histories have come and gone. That means there must be some truth in that, which is the reason why we are searching for that truth. If we are to take it as history and start comparing him with other histories, His teaching was that God loves us and He encouraged us to love one another, taught people to love one another. He also taught that there was a kingdom in heaven but it had come on earth, teaching people to practise it. He also told people that there would be a judgement in the end, but that message seems too remote for people to understand it He also taught that God forgives, maybe that has given people a sense of comfort that after all we will be forgiven. His teachings showed not to be subversive, but it is surprising why His teachings were hated to such an extent that they tried to make up stories to condemn Him to death until they succeeded in making up the stories. They arrested Him and handed Him over to one who was the governor to be tried.

Although Pilate said he could not find any fault with Him, they were furious that He must be sentenced to death until Pilate gave in. He was killed by means of being crucified on the cross, He was buried, but to their surprise, He rose from the dead on the third day. Those who were very much against Him tried to spread a word that it was just a delusion, because there was no such a thing that had happened in their history. That is the reason why Jesus had to stay forty days after His resurrection; it was to prove that the resurrection was not a delusion. Still His enemies to this day would like to make people believe that there is no such a thing in living memory

(Webarchieve.nationalarchieves.gov.uk: tainted aspects of culture) Sometimes culture leads people to do things that are un-holy. That is what Christianity tries to correct. Some of the things that may be used by culture as medicine may be used excessively, and not orderly. Christianity says there must be some training. As the environment gets polluted, so does the culture, it get polluted sometimes, as we strive to get a polluted free environment, so do we also strive to have to get free polluted cultural aspects.

JESUS CHRIST IS THE ONLY WAY TO GOD, AND NO ANY OTHER WAY:

Jesus is the only way to heaven. The only way we can also go to heaven is to accept Him in our hearts. There are no two roads to heaven, (Matthew 16:16)(KJV) Peter said "you are the Christ the Son of God". What Peter said was that Jesus was the divine, and the long waited Messiah. If Jesus asked you this question today how were you going to answer, is He your Lord and Messiah? It is not enough to say Jesus Christ is the Messiah, but to be convicted deep down in your heart. If you were to compare Christianity and other religions, you would focus on Jesus as the answer When Jesus came on earth, some people were caught unawares. This book pleads with the modern readers not to be caught unawares. It is a blessing to be forewarned, so that you are not found wanting, when the time comes. (John 1:4, and 9. John 10:30) (KJV) Jesus said "I and my Father are one" Jesus was saying that he is not the same as his Father, but that they are one. (John 14:9) (KJV) "Jesus aid unto Philip I have been so long time with you, and yet you have not known me, Philip? He that has seen me has seen the Father, and how can you say then show us the Father?" God had seen that we had gone astray because of the original sin, so He decided to save us from that sin, so He had tome in person. That is the reason why He came as Jesus, when He departed, He left us with the Holy Spirit that is why we ask for the revelation in order for us to understand the "trinity", and Jesus is God revealed to us. The reason why Jesus was crucified is that they never understood him; shall we keep on misunderstanding Him? If those people who are saying that those who follow Him are narrow minded, then that means we have to start looking at the whole and start asking questions some say He was blasphemy that is why they killed Him. If they killed Him, where is He now if they say He rose from the dead, where is He now? If they say He is in heaven then we have to start looking at the narrow mindedness. How can He be in heaven if He has no relationship with heaven? (John 10:30) (KJV)What does Jesus mean when He says "I and my Father are one" (John 14:9) (KJV) There is a Holiness and greatness which is not understood.(John 14:6) (KJV) "I am the way the truth and the life" (John 1:14) (KJV), and the word became flesh and dwelt among us, and we saw His glory, and is no other than the Son of God.

JESUS CHRIST AS LORD GAVE HIMSELF UP FOR OUR CAUSE, WE HAVE TO GIVE OURSELVES UP IN ORDER TO MEET HALFWAY:

Christians, society and the governments must work together in order to have a good quality of life which is found in working together in harmony. We are advised to surrender our lives to Jesus Christ because He is faithful and is so loving, that He gave His own life for you and me, how can He let us down at this stage. Jesus gave us an example of being the first to rise from the dead, by this we are assured of the resurrection of our souls for eternal life if we follow Him. Society will always want to hide behind multiculturalism, yet multiculturalism has been there since the days of Judeo Christianity, when there was a transition from Judaism to Christanity. In them they already have that mentality of wanting to see the persecution of believers. The aim of writing on culture and Christianity is to try to bridge the gap that exist between culture and Christianity, but it still seems there is a dividing line between them. What causes this is what researchers are trying to find out, and to come up with a long term solution. In (Luke 22:46) (KJV) Jesus tells His disciples, the only way was to keep watch by praying, because there are so many forces that want to sway you from being attached to your Father. Jesus suffered on the cross, died, and rose from the dead, which means He conquered death for us, but this does not mean that those forces have gone away; they are still trying to steal us away from our heavenly Father, like what can be seen in cultural diversity. If you communicate to one another regularly, you will get to understand each other fully, the applies to the Lord, you get to understand Him better if you are familiar with Him by talking to Him more often, the reader is advised to put this into practice. Spiritually surrender yourself to Him, and He is kind enough to lead you in your life. Jesus' life is full of evidence that it is better for us to put our trust in Him. We must always be humble enough to be able to confess our sins as it is the only way to build our relationship with Him, as He came to show us the way and give an example of living, He expects us to know Him better now than before.

CULTURE SOMETIMES DEVIATES FROM GOD.

(Chris Russell: Bible tools .org. Things that cause us to Drift Spiritually) Sometimes what causes us to deviate could be, we tend to lapse spiritually. The devil is very cunning, he can make us to have something which may occupy our minds in such a way that we may not realise it. By the time we realise we will have drifted far, far away from where we were supposed to be. In our lives, the devil might bring so many attractions just to deviate our attention from the truth. Look at your life calendar, there are so many things that may appear of importance in life, yet when those things May have very little to do with the upkeep of our souls. Sometimes we tend to let things in our lives rule over our lives. Let us ask for divine intervention, because if we try to use our blood and flesh to fight this war we are not going to win it. Our cultural values should not conflict with God's wishes which we should always follow so that our relationship with Him is that of Father to son. The good thing about following God's will is that His laws are not meant to inflict pain on us. For us not to be taken unawares we must always be vigilant and do the will of God always, so that we are always protected with His grace and mercy.(Ephesians 5:16) We must keep our standards high and always trying to be doing good all the time of our lives, because if we cannot the devil is always looking for chances to deviate us from the will of God.

(Christianity Today) *accessed 27.2.2020* sometimes culture might affect the way we understand scriptures, we must not come to the scriptures with preconceived interpretations. It appears the way we look at scriptures we only look around us without asking, but what does God say? When two religions are trying to come together to form one thing, they will always conflict because of differences in their beliefs.(Sage Journals) That is, we will be coming to it with obedience and asking for revelations.

THE HOPES OF SOME PEOPLE ARE VESTED IN THEIR CULTURE:

(Wurtz E.onlinelibrary.wiley.com: intercultural: communication) Sometimes we are immersed in false hope that we sometimes think that aging might be postponed or that death can be dodged. People behave the way they behave because of the culture they have assimilated; it could be organisational or professional culture. The cultures become extended because they will rely on extended networks involving the relationship as starting with grandparents, parents, siblings, aunts and uncles cousins, and brothers.

THE PEOPLE'S LOYALTY IS VESTED IN THEIR CULTURE EXPECTING TO BE GUIDED TO THEIR DESTINATION:

For anything, that you do to succeed there must be some sort of loyalty. If there is loyalty that means there is trust for one another, or each other. Loyalty means of good quality means faithful to each other and means honourable means discharging your duties legally and happily. Be loyal to anything it in return it will move smoothly. That is the reason why culture survives, because they teach the next generation that they cannot do without, this is implanted to them at a very young age. In normal circumstances, people are grilled at a very young age that a culture is very essential for their livelihood. As they grow they are not let off the hook, refreshers are always, they are made to focus on what is before them. When one is involved in a business, which involves employing people of different characters, it will prosper if the employee is loyal to that business. When a person becomes an employer, the first thing to do is to find ways of making the employees loyal. Make the employees feel that they belong to the business, so they must have a sense of belonging, value them so they feel they valued. Make them feel they have a future in that business.

HOW PEOPLE UNDERSTAND THEIR CULTURE AND OTHER PEOPLE'S CULTURES:

There are so many different cultures, and the world is fast becoming multicultural. There is need to understand some other different cultures in order to be able to accommodate other cultures in a multicultural society. To do this you have to evaluate your own culture, compare with what other cultures value, your personal biases and give other cultures a chance. Be accommodative and more tolerant to other cultures than yours in order to be able to work together. Do not look down upon their cultures or neither should you down upon your, Just take them as equals. Take other cultures on their own standards. Many different people have many different backgrounds. Learn their backgrounds, and note that they did not choose to have that culture or that background but that it only came to them as inheritance, of which they have no control on them, it will make things easy, if you do not try to make them change.

CHAPTER 4

HOW GOD SEES CULTURE AS:

When reading the Bible, which is the word of God we have to have a clear vision, otherwise we might be visualising it wrongly, we need to have a clear vision. (J. Gresham Machen) There has always been tension between cultures and Christianity. It appears even up to this present day Christians are unable to tell exactly what relationship, or what differences are there between culture and Christianity. Since the fear of the Lord is the beginning of knowledge, it is better to have that knowledge from the Lord, and then there is no problem between knowledge and Piety, they will have good relationship and no problem between knowledge and piety and no difference between scientific and academic. They all relate to research and investigation and exploration the result will contribute to the advancement of humanity that means without a clear-cut message, who is leading who now? If we are still groping, is it advisable to go back to the drawing board? Being saved is the main goal; now let us ask for divine revelation and to be saved at the same time, because there is no point in having the knowledge without being saved. For us to saved means to reflect on your deeds, if you see they are not pleasing to God, then you have to repent and ask for forgiveness, our Lord is faithful enough to forgive us.

CHRISTIANS SHOULD KNOW WHICH SIDE OF CULTURE THEY CAN STAND IN ORDER TO ACHIEVE THEIR GOAL:

The reason why the church seems to be drawing a line between it and culture is that the church fears to be diluted into culture and end up being lukewarm it their Christianity. But each of these two opposing forces would like to take an upper hand in influencing society. It appears Christianity is unable to against the forces of darkness that are against it. The church should be well equipped to fight against these force, that is, they should ask to be filled by the Holy Spirit which will give it the courage to stand against these forces. Christians know that the best way to know it better is to be close to it, but then they fear that to be too much into you may end up being diluted yourself, and then you have compromised your Christianity. The politicians seem to be leaned closely to culture than to Christianity that is the reason why culture appears to be gaining momentum because of the backing from politicians.

SOMETIMES CHRISTIANS SHOULD LOOK AT CULTURE CLOSELY IN ORDER TO KNOW WHICH DIRECTION TO FOLLOW:

Paul says, "Be not conformed to this world, but be transformed by the renewing of your mind"(Romans 12:2) (KJV) we have to stay in obedience to God's will so that we are not carried away. "Do not let the world around you squeeze you into its own mould." Jesus even said it when He prayed to the Father he said Father Keep them in the world but fill them with the Holy Spirit so that they can be able to transform the world. (Luke 17:26) (KJV) Let the Holy Spirit lead us to knowing Him better because there is not going to be any new different signs that He is coming. The problem that could be faced by Christians if they would stand in culture is that culture sometimes indulges into ungodly actions, so if Christians are standing in culture, they will be compelled to do these things, which are ungodly. (Luke 17:26) (KJV) Jesus is warning against indulging into something that would draw out spirits backward, for the time comes of His judgement, there will be no time for repentance. Sometimes the devil brings things which appear like they are good yet he knows that they us into sinning, so it up to every Christian to weigh things for themselves.

CHRISTIANS MUST STRIVE AND BE TACTFUL IN ORDER TO ACHIEVE THEIR GOAL IN CULTURE:

Christianity slowly lost its influence in culture despite its rapid conversion growth. The different social institutions of culture and those who have their faith in culture work together for a common goal. (Stanford Encyclopaedia of Philosophy) The beliefs are what are affecting (H. Richard Niebuhr's "Christ and Culture") the relationship that is there between culture and Christianity has always been a subject of debate. Jesus was always in conflict with the Pharisees. The Pharisees were always thinking that Jesus wanted to do away with their culture. So currently, this subject has to be looked at with caution, when dealing with this, we have always to seek some Biblical guidance, if we are to go along with it the way it should, because the subject is very sensitive on every side you might want to look at it. (John 2:15-16) (KJV) Sometimes we get carried away and forget that our bodies are God's Temple like what Jesus discovered when He got to the temple, they had shifted from the Holiness of the temple to make it a den of thieves. Should we see a church as a place of personal contact? It has to be treated as sacred; the same applies to our bodies they should be kept pure from any kind of blemish. Let us ask the Lord to guide us to always be in spirit whenever we come to His place of worship. Jesus' anger here was a divine anger, we should be very careful when dealing with those who might be mixing Culture with Christianity, we should handle the situation with caution, because we may end up with anger that is unholy, and the whole purpose of trying to correct it may be lost. Let us not forget that these two exist together, the kingdom of darkness and the kingdom of light, it is up to us to choose which one we want to take as Christians. Jesus Himself did not take us from this world. (John 17:11 and 21) (KJV) Jesus is saying for now we must not appear as heavenly beings while we are still on earth but to try to take ourselves as the salt of the earth by trying by all means to bring them to Christ following His example, we must show the world by our deeds which are Christ like, and He will do the rest. Let us pray for one another for that is the start of being Christ like.

(DR. Bruce Riley Ashford, "Every Square Inch") (Ephesians 6:10-20) (KJV) between culture and Christianity, sometimes there seem to be some antagonism between the two which requires us to search why it is like that, no one culture wants to bow down to the other. It appears culture wants to take advantage of multi-culturalism. Ephesians states clearly that there are some forces headed by fallen angels, who are always against the will of God. There is nowhere we can fight these forces with our own flesh, but to always ask God to shield us under his arms. Since culture is our way of living, the devil wants to take advantage of that. When culture is being corrected, the devil will say look culture is being tempered with, yet some way of living may be corrected and move on without killing anything. In the garden of Gethsemane Jesus fought a spiritual battle for us to be like him we have to fight these spiritual battles, because sometimes we are being tempted not to fight these battles. Our model of prayer should be likened to Jesus' when He prayed in (Luke 22:44) (KJV) he was in agony, what model are we following of prayer, sometimes we meet with some situations that require us to be in agony, are we? It is true that Jesus had sweat that was drops of blood, it is true that under great stress, small capillaries break and mix blood with sweat glands.

ALTHOUGH CULTURES ARE DIFFERENT, THERE ARE SOME SIMILARITIES IN THEM:

In this modern day because so many nationalities are coming together and so many different cultures are meeting in work environments, so it is advisable to take similarities in culture and try to build from there other than dwelling on differences. This means that these minute differences will disappear and give way to a multicultural society.

CHAPTER 5

THERE IS A HIDDEN PERSECUTION OF BELIEVERS WORLDWIDE:

It appears Christianity has suffered for a very long period of time. The reason is that it did not spread to all the countries of the world at once. We learn from history that immediately after Jesus had ascended and the apostles were trying to spread Christianity. That is the time when people were resisting finding it difficult to change their way of life to Christianity. Where Christianity has been for a long time, people seem to have adapted to the way of life of Christianity, and able to have found that it is not a terrorist organisation and have accommodated it in their lives. As it spreads to countries where it was not before the persecution persists, hence there is still persecution of believers. This persecution is still going on even 2 000 years after Christ has ascended places like the Middle East are still being killed for belonging to Christianity. Millions of Christians are still being displaced, there is a lot of exodus still taking place in these countries.

(Open doors uk.org: Trends: persecution of believers worldwide) these days Christians are being treated unfavourably, some are even being killed because of their faith. That means all the Christians are suffering because Christianity means one body. Even governments are putting more laws that try to restrict Christianity movement. Even though in some countries it may appear like things are stable for Christians, there are some countries which are still under great persecution for practising Christianity. Countries in the Middle East like Iraq and Syria in the present day it is very dangerous to be seen practising Christianity. That is what it is in this book that they are saying that Christianity is killing their culture. There are organisations such as "Help the Persecuted" which are trying to stand with those who are suffering under the name of Christ in these countries. Let all Christians unite in prayer for this persecution to stop in the name of Christ. We know that Christ Himself did not promise us easy going, but we also understand that He has got the power to make His word spread for His own glory. The wish of all Christians is make sure that His word reaches everyone for His word is a light to every soul.

THE EARLY BELIEVERS SUFFERED A HARSH PERSECUTION:

(1 Peter) (KJV) "When you suffer for doing what is right, remember that following Christ is a costly commitment. When persecuted for your faith, rejoice that you have been counted worth to suffer for Christ. He suffered for us; as His followers, we should expect nothing less." (1 Peter) (KJV) reminds us that our faith is strengthened refined by trial. When trials come, remain faithful to God you will get a reward in the end. Early Christians suffered from three angles that are from the Jews, because Christianity came from Judaism. The Jews were saying you are teaching heresy, from the Romans because they were the ones ruling, they said you want to establish a parallel government, from the pagans because they were saying why worshiping a different God than their shrines. The persecution of Christians in the New Testament is good for us because it shows us that we are following the footsteps of our Saviour. On the crucifixion of Jesus, it appears no one wants to take the responsibility, the Jews say they were not the ones ruling, while the Romans say they had found Him not guilty, but the Jews then cried out saying crucify Him, let his blood come on us and our children, (food for thought). When the Jewish people persecuted Christians they thought that they were defending the laws of God in the Old Testament, disregarding the fact that Jesus was the Son of God. There are some saints who are filled with the Holy Spirit that they are happy to be persecuted for the name of Christ.

THE JOHANNINE COMMUNITY EVADE PERSECUTION
IN ORDER TO PRESERVE CHRISTIANITY:

(Bibleodyssey.org.Johannene Community Evade Persecution) This community did not leave Judaism quickly or leaving the synagogue quickly, wanting to have a gradual change in such a way that by the time they would realise, Christianity would evangelised many people to the extent that it would be difficult to eradicate. By the time, they were expelled from the synagogue, they able to function as a new group called Christians.

(Church History timeline Christianity .com/Church: What were early Christians like? AD 1-300) Early Christianity covers the period from its origins (c-30-36) until the first council of Nicaea (325), this period covers the Apostolic Age, which is (30-100), and the Ante-Nicene-Period 9C-100-325). The first Christians were Jewish Christians. Many Christians were by birth or by conversion that is, as proselytes, these were of the belief that Christ died on the cross for us and rose from the dead, and is alive today and watching over us. This belief grew so popular that the Christian religion became the world's religion. As this grew, that is how they left the Jewish customs and embarked on Christianity.

THE EARLY CHRISTIANS WERE PERSECUTED, BUT THEY FOUND SOME WAYS AND
MEANS TO EVADE THAT PERSECUTION IN ORDER TO PRESERVE CHRISTIANITY:

(Christianity Today.com/Issues: Persecution in early church) The church allowed flight in order to escape persecution; some of them went into hiding in order for things to die down before they would come into the open. Those who would not go into hiding were martyr, and were made saints. Some accepted martyrdom, as Christ had died on the cross, as He had come on earth to give an example, so they said it was fitting to follow His example.

THE PERSECUTION OF EARLY BELIEVERS HELPED TO SPREAD THE CHURCH:

(Acts 8:1-8) (KJV), after the Pentecost, the Apostles were filled with the Holy Spirit, but it was not all plain sailing. There started persecution of the church in Jerusalem. As they tried to evade persecution, some went to Judea, some to Samaria. That is the time when Stephen was killed by stoning, and Saul guarding clothes of those stoning Stephen. Saul was leading in persecuting those found talking about Christ or those believing in His name or those practising Christianity: Jesus had said it when He had given the great commission that they would start in Jerusalem, Judea, and Samaria, then to all the ends of the world. So when Philip went to Samaria, the second part of Jesus' great commission was fulfilled. God works in mysterious ways, you will have to be uncomfortable in order to move. We may not want it, but if they are God's ways, we have to follow them without choice. Sometimes we go through very hard times, when it happens we start going in a different direction. What happened to those early believers should always remind us when that also happens to us. Let us always bear in mind that this is still happening in our present day, only that we never give it a thought, only calling it misfortunes. If their persecution helped to spread the gospel, why should our persecution today not spread the gospel?

4 BC: Birth of Jesus Christ of Nazareth.

27 AD: Beginning of Jesus Christ's public preaching. The population of the Roman Empire was 33,000,000 at the time. (50% of them were slaves).

30 AD: Crucifixion, resurrection and ascension of Christ. His commandment is given. "Go therefore and make disciples of all nations" (Matthew 28:19-20) (KJV). Jesus appears to the nation for 40 days after the resurrection. The reason for making this appearance for forty days is to confirm the fact that He rose from the dead, he wanted to prove beyond any doubt that He rose from the dead. This He proved by showing the nail marks in His hands and feet, because many who doubted were saying that this was just a delusion. This seems like it has also affected the present generation who still doubt the resurrection. For the understanding of the

resurrection, requires prayers that He gives s understanding and faith of His revelation of the resurrection. Those who still doubt the resurrection are advised to follow Thomas's example, who doubted at first but later believed. His resurrection was confirmed at Pentecost when the Holy Spirit descended and 3000 Jewish proselytes became Christians.

34 AD: Stephen was murdered by stoning and the persecution of Christians begins. At the stoning of Stephen, it showed clearly that he was filled with the Holy Spirit. The motive of this book is to plead with the reader to always ask for the Holy Spirit for guidance into the truth. When guided by the Holy Spirit, there will be no doubting of the resurrection. There are so many who sacrificed their lives for Christianity to be how it is today. As Christianity is going through a hidden persecution, are we making a sacrifice for its survival?

35 AD: The gospel spreads to Judea and Samaria. (Acts 9:31), the church throughout Judea and Samaria enjoyed a time of peace and was strengthened. Living in fear of the Lord and encouraged by the Holy Spirit, it increased in numbers. The fear of the Lord is not a fear of someone who is bully to you, but the fear of the Lord means that we are establishing a closer relationship with Him. The fear of the Lord is the beginning of wisdom. Because of the persecution the people were forced to flee their homes in Jerusalem, they started preaching where ever they went, fulfilling the second part of Jesus' commandment. Saul guarded the clothes of those who killed Stephen by stoning him.

36-40 AD: Cornelius and many other gentiles were converted to Christianity, Acts 10:1-48. This has shown that God receives anyone who believes in Him without first going through Jewish culture.

44 AD: Killing of Christians, including Harold Agrippa, and James, Peter escapes from prison, Christians were exiled. Under all that persecution, they were strengthened by the Holy Spirit, which made them happy to die for the sake of Christianity.

50 AD: Paul preaches in Macedonia, Achaea and Asia, Jewish Christians exiled from Rome, (Acts 16:6).

60 AD: First Christians in Dalmatia Illyria (Yugoslavia)

61 AD: Start of the Celtic Church.

63 AD: Mark was killed in Bocelli, near Alexandra.

(Note) 64 AD: Started the great persecution of believers, Nero's reason for doing that was that the Christians were the ones who caused the great fire of Rome. For that reason, that's when Peter and Paul was martyr, this includes thousands of Christians. Nero did the killing of Christians to cover up the great fire of Rome: some Christians were torn up by dogs, some thrown into the fire. This shows what tension is always there between Christianity and non-Christians

66 AD: Most Jews were killed in an anti-Jewish operation where many Jews were massacred in Egypt: 50 000 in Alexandra, and 60 000 in other places.

67 AD: Many Jews organised a riot, but it was supressed by so many soldiers.

69 AD: Many Jews in diaspora were Christians numbering about 4 000 000.

70 AD: 4 legions with Titus destroyed Jerusalem killing about 600 000 in Judea while 10 000 were crucified: 90 000 taken to Rome as slaves. The destruction of Rome was predicted in prophecy so many years back. When Jews ran away, they spread the gospel where ever they went. The centre for the spread of the gospel was Antioch.

71 AD: Many Christians were martyr by being thrown to beasts or any other cruel way of killing.

80 AD: Christian centre was transferred to Ephesus; the first Christians reached France, Italy and Tunisia.

81 AD: The second Roman imperial mass persecution by Domitian (81-86 AD) Christians were not paying a tax known as "the two-drachma tax" for some time, Domitian took this as an excuse for killing Christians. Dionysius the Arcopagite first bishop of Athens was martyr through fire,

this includes Timothy the student of Paul, had become the bishop of Ephesus.

There was introduced a system of worshipping the emperor. Those who refused were murdered, this involved about 40 000 Christians. This persecution was very violent, though short. This spread all over Rome and Italy. This was also the time when John was exiled to Patmos, while he was there, led by the Holy Spirit wrote the Apocalypse.

90 AD: West Germany's first Christians (West Germany, today's name).

98 AD: This was the reign of Trojan, the 3rd Roman imperial mass persecution, lasted from (98-117AD. The accusation being that they refused to worship the emperor, and also refusing to sacrifice to Roman gods. Simeon Jesus Christ's brother was also murdered, he was bishop of Jerusalem, was crucified in 107 AD: As well as Ignatius, 2nd bishop of Antioch who was killed by being thrown to beasts in Rome.

100 AD: 60 years after the death of Christ, it was 0.6% Christian as world population and 28% had heard about the gospel and the scripture was translated into 6 languages.

First Christians in Monaco, in Sri-Lanka (then Ceylon), in Saudi Arabia, in Romania (then the Roman province of Dacia).

115 AD: Bishop of Antioch, Saint Ignatius was martyred.

117 AD: Hadrian continued the persecution of Christians (117-138 AD), his persecution was a bit moderate. In all those persecutions, Christianity grew stronger; many souls were won even from higher social levels. Encouragement preaching and speeches made Christianity to stand fast.

132 AD: The Romans destroyed Jerusalem for the second time, after there had been a second revolt by the Jews under Barkokhba most of the Palestinian's population died, few escaped.

136 AD: Hadrian erected the temple of Zeus instead of the temple of Jerusalem.

138 AD: The persecution did not stop, spilled into the reign of Antonius (138-161). This emperor did not directly persecute Christians but put stiff laws that Christians were failing to cope, hence many Christians became martyr.

150 AD: First Christians in Portugal, Anchialas, and DeVito's along the Black sea.

156 AD: Bishop of Sanmina Polycarp was murdered.

"Note" 161 AD: Marcus Aurelius continued the 4th Roman imperial Mass persecution (161-180 AD). This one proved to be more- cruel than Nero. This is the time when Justin the Christian writer became martyr. His victims suffered incredible torcher. The persecution was continued by his son, for them to persecute the early believers or Christianity, they claimed that they were defending their religion or their culture. It has to be bone in mind that that those are very much in culture are still at the defence of the culture but in a very tactful way, that it may not be noticed as it was before.

"Note" When Christianity faces persecution currently, it is not the same persecution, but done in such a way that it may be difficult to call it persecution.

174 AD: Austria had its first Christians.

180 AD: Although Christianity was being supressed that is the time when it spread to nearly all the provinces of the Roman Empire. That is the time when Christianity was starting missionary schools and educational schools. This opening of missionary schools spread to as far as India in only 9 years.

190 AD: Christianity spread in North Africa very rapidly.

193 AD: As if it was a wealthy heritage, this persecution of believers was passed from one emperor to the other. When the 5th Roman imperial persecution was passed on to Saptami's Severus, he reigned from (193-211 AD). He passed a law in 202 AD, which prohibited proselytes. He had

very harsh laws, these affected the countries of North Africa the most, and most Christians were martyr through crucifixion or were burnt in fire. Many people suffered for us to inherit this seeming mild Christianity, which was not like that before. Their persecution was almost on daily basis, from 202- 211 AD.

197 AD: It appears this spilling of blood spread to every nation, for no nation was spared for the martyrdom wrote Tertullian.

200 AD: Christianity grew 3.4% in 160 years after Jesus Christ had gone, and 32% of the world population had heard of the scripture, or of Christ.

205 AD: The spread of the gospel all over the world reaching as far as Athens and Greece, as written by Clement of Alexandria.

210 AD: The gospel spreads to as far as Qatar that is in Persian province evidenced in 224 AD.

225 AD: The gospel spreads to Tigris and Euphrates, this area at one time had 20 bishops. This is in the Caspian Sea and Bahrain.

235 AD: Maxi minus led the 6th Roman empirical persecution (235-238 AD). Many Christians were killed, Origen escaped by hiding.

"Check and rewrite up to the word world" 240 AD: Christianity was perused during the time of Bishop Gregory that by the time of 27 AD Christianity spread to 95% of the world.

249 AD: Decius led the 7th persecution which lasted from (249-251 AD), but in that short period he tried to destroy Christianity systematically. He wanted to see Christianity completely wiped off. His reason for this harsh persecution was that Christianity was causing the fall of the Roman Empire. Many church leaders were martyr; many were dreading to be Christians because of this harsh persecution.

250 AD: In spite of all this persecution, the church grew rapidly.

251 AD: There were so many needy people so Christianity continued to grow.

252AD: An outbreak of a plague epidemic killed 25% of the Roman population, the church helped by sourcing medication, in some areas about 50% of the population died.

253 AD: Valerian continued the 8th Roman imperial persecution which lasted from (253-260 AD). He killed many Christians including the Bishop Cyprian of Carthage.

260 AD: The persecution being there, the Christianity population still grew to 40% of the Roman Empire.

270 AD: The first Basilicas (Square Christian Churches) were built (270-275 AD) 9th Roman Imperial persecution under Aurelian.

287 AD: Christianity is declared the nation's official religion, mass acceptance especially in Armenia.

295 AD: David versa hears the gospel in India.

300 AD: 9 generations after Christ, the world is 4.4% Christian, 35% have heard the gospel, spreading to Afghanistan.

303 AD: 10th and last Roman Imperial persecution, destruction of all church buildings, and destruction of scriptures. 500 000 Christians were murdered in 9 years of persecution (284-305 AD)this was the worst of the persecutions under Diocletian, the harshest destruction organised throughout the whole Empire "Check and rewrite up to Corinth" Christians rant into forests and caves 15 000 Christians were put to death. St. George was killed in Egypt, and Corinth.

310 AD: Galatia is still 70% idolaters.

"Take note up to Christianity"313 AD: Constantine tolerated Christianity, and issued laws to legalise Christianity.

319 AD: Because of the laws of Constantine, pagan sacrifices were outlawed throughout the Empire.

"Note up to Empire"330 AD: The Christian population world over, 10 generations after Christ, Christianity rose to 12% of the world population, 36% had heard of the gospel, while the scripture had been translated into 10 different languages, and also the capital of the empire was translocated to Constantinople339 AD: But in some areas, persecution continues such as in Persia, stretched from (339-379 AD), this was carried out during Sasanian's reign up to 640 AD when it was conquered by Islam.

340 AD: Bishoprics in Egypt number 100.

345 AD: In eastern Syria the persecution continues.

350 AD: Meroe's reign started to disintegrate, 3 succeeding nations were Christians spreading to as far as Ireland.

361 AD: The pagan religion kept on dying a natural death in the Roman Empire.

378 AD: Spreading of Christianity to India and Britain, but statistics show that about 1 900 000 had become martyrs since 30 AD.

380 AD: 50% of Antioch is Christians. Theodosius recognises Christianity as a national religion, many becoming Christians.

395 AD: Split of the Roman Empire, Western and Eastern empires. The Eastern half was ruled by Constantinople.

400 AD: The world population 17.1% Christian; 39% have heard of the gospel. This happened 12 generations after Christ: scripture translated into 11 different languages.

"Check up to Visgoths" 409 AD: Iberian Peninsula is invaded Arian Visigoths.

438 AD: Christians had increased in number to be able to conquer the Roman Empire.

With all these forces fighting against Christianity, but Christianity survived. All those forces wanted Christianity to be wiped off, but instead it expanded to become the world's religion. By the year 260 AD Christianity had expanded to be 40% of the Roman Empire. As the church expanded paganism declined.

The reason why Christianity suffered the most is that as it grew contemporary with paganism, paganism wanted Christianity to worship and sacrifice to Roman gods, when Christians knew well that there was a living God whom they wanted pagans to worship. That did not go well with both sides, pagans wondering why Christians were refusing to sacrifice to their gods

This has degenerated into this present age where the atheists are trying by all hidden means to see the extinction of Christianity from the face of the earth. At the height of tension between pagan and Christianity, we have examples like Polycarp who refused to bow down to pagan gods, as a result of his refusal; he was burnt alive as a martyr of Christ. Punishments such as this mostly happened under the reign of Nero.

Since the Romans had colonised many nations there were so many cults under the Roman Empire which means the Romans had to pay more attention to so many cults. As they dealt with so many cults, meant the persecution for Christianity lulled for a time. Christians never changed their behaviour of being a non-subversive organisation to this date.

THE EARLY CHRISTIAN BELIEVERS SUFFERED PERSECUTION BECAUSE PEOPLE HATED THEIR MOVEMENT:

(DR. Sophie Lunn-Rocliffe) During the reign of Nero in the year 64 AD a fire broke out in Rome which destroyed most of the city. Without proper investigations, Nero Quickly put the blame on Christianity; hence the persecution of Christians began. There is a rumour that is still alive to date with his dislike to Christianity; he himself started the fire for him to have a base where to put the blame on Christianity. He gave orders that Christians should be rounded up. Some of them were burnt alive some were thrown to dogs alive and were torn to pieces. The time that followed, Christians suffered at the hands of emperors when the middle of the third century the persecution was at its highest pick. The peace we could be enjoying today was bought by a lot of blood. This teaches us that we have to try as much as we can to preserve this Christianity because there are some who preserved it by their blood. With the fact that emperors were persecuting Christians gave those who hated Christianity in the first a scapegoat to put all the blame on Christianity. Pagans were happy to say Christians must worship pagan gods, when Christians knew b so well that there was a living God, so refusing to sacrifice to the Roman gods was a serious crime, punishable by death. Many Christian faiths were tested that way. Let a Christian of today be warned that these persecutions are there today but they are now very tactful, and they still test our faith, are we not going to be caught unawares? As has been said that God works in mysterious ways, the Roman Empire had many cults to deal with such that it was becoming difficult to pay attention to Christianity hence there was a lull in the persecution of Christianity.

THE PERSECUTION OF CHRISTIAN BELIEVERS WORLDWIDE TAUGHT US TO BE VIGILANT ALL THE TIME:

Currently, there are countries where Christianity is forbidden, so those who are trying to introduce it are being harassed or persecuted as those of the first century. It is for us to be with them in spirit because they are suffering for the religion in which we believe. We have examples of countries like North Korea, Afghanistan, Somalia, Libya, Pakistan, Sudan to name just a few. Some Christians in these countries have decided to go into hiding so they may not be killed or persecuted. The persecution of Christians has not gone away because as Christians were persecuted in the first century, they are still suffering persecution as before but only that as time changes and also the persecution has also changed tactic, the reason being that the devil is very tactful as to do it in such a way that it will not be noticed but in the end Christianity is suffering. Christianity has so many divisions like denominations. Christians start fighting for denominations Instead of fighting in the survival of Christianity they are fighting for denominations. Even though Christians today seem to be free to practise their Christianity freely, it is not all Christians who would say they are free to practise their faith freely. There are countries like North Korea, there is a very small minority about 1.2% who are faithful to Christianity, but are facing hardships, like if you are caught practising it, it is life imprisonment or in some cases facing murder (Open DoorsUK.org./north-Korea-prison) they are trying to work with those persecuted. No one is allowed to take pictures of how they are suffering, so no one is able to offer any help to those persecuted or imprisoned. Anybody who believes in any other higher authority than Kim family the dictator is considered an enemy of the state. Kim and his family are worshipped as gods, if you think of worshipping any other than them, you must be imprisoned. This is not like it is history that believers were persecuted during the time of the Apostles after the ascension of Jesus, but that it is still happening today, let all Christians unite and pray for the freedom of our brothers and sisters worldwide who are still living such a life today, our Lord has got all the power.

AT THE HEIGHT OF HARD TIMES, CHRISTIANS EMPLOYED STRATEGIES OF OPERATION TO SURVIVE:

During the time of persecution Christianity survived or flourished because Christians employed new strategies of operation. That is a very big lesson to Christians of today who are sitting back and crying "foul" that multiculturalism is killing Christianity, without following the footsteps of the apostles who, the more they were persecuted the more Christianity expanded. There is no time that Christianity has been easy. Even when Jesus came to earth to set an example, it was not easy, not plain sailing, never at any time. If everything was fine He would not have been crucified. Christianity received a big boost during the reign of Constantine when he legitimised Christianity. When Christianity was at the height of persecuting, like it was a generous providence Constantine recognised

Christianity and made it an official imperial religion. This was a historical turnabout of the Christian religion. This came as a relief, as Christianity had suffered for over four centuries. We can only conclude that God works in mysterious ways. He arranges His times without consulting anybody. When the time comes which He has set, everything will begin to take their shape. When Jesus was on earth for slightly over three years He dis start Christianity. But after He had left, Christianity started as a movement but only to grow the world's most recognised religion.

CHAPTER 6

CHRISTIANITY SURVIVES WHEN PAGANISM WAS DECLINING:

The expansion of Christianity at the height of its persecution means that there could be some inspirational providence behind it. There is good cause for this book to appeal to its reader to try to weigh between Christianity and paganism.

Although the style of persecution has changed, there are still some hidden forces fighting for the downfall of Christianity. Paganism was declining because it did not have the life of the people at heart. Unlike Christianity has got love for the people, and has got their welfare at heart. The religious movement sometimes divine intervention, because most of the time it obedient to God.

THERE CAME A TIME WHEN PAGANISM WAS DECLINING WHEN CHRISTIANITY WAS EXPANDING:

Christians based their faith on the risen Christ who is a true God unlike paganism who worshiped gods made by hands of man. One of the factors that made Christianity to grow was that Constantine was converted into Christianity, so paganism was shunned for a while. The reason why Christianity would succeed while paganism was declining was that, since Jesus promised in Matthew 16:18 when He said to Peter that "on you I will build my church", this means Jesus Himself sustains the church, something He continues doing even in the present day and in future ours is to put our trust and faith in Him. Also before He left, He strongly commanded them to stay in Jerusalem and wait for the promise of the Father; the spirit who will guide us through our lives and to sustain the church. "While paganism was declining," means that, while the church was being helped by the Holy Spirit, no one was helping Paganism. In that people are able to choose and separate good from bad. This must be happening even to this present day people must be able to choose and separate light from darkness. Light and darkness do not stay together in any circumstances. Although there is a hidden persecution these days, people must be able to separate light from darkness, good from bad. But where ever the people have a choice, people tend to choose the wrong thing.

BEGINNINGS OF CHRISTIANITY:

Christianity developed in Judea in the mid-first century AD based on the teachings of Jesus, and later on the writings of Paul of Tarsus. Originally, Christianity was an unorganised sect that promised personal salvation after death. Salvation was possible through believing in Jesus Christ as the Son of God, the same God that the Jews believed in. So it was difficult to convince people to leave the God they were also preaching about. The difference was that, the Christians believed that salvation was for all. So Christianity started gaining popularity throughout the Roman Empire. The main reason for it to develop out of Judaism was that it was inspired by God. Jesus was a Jew; during His time on earth He never started the Christian movement. His words were, "you will receive power", that is the power then that enabled them to start the Christian movement, and enabling today's Christians to sustain Christianity.

THE GOSPEL OF JOHN WAS WRITTEN IN ORDER TO SHOW THAT JESUS OF NAZARETH WAS CHRIST:

(Cliff's notes.com/literature: to show that Jesus of Nazareth was Christ) The Gospel of John is the latest-written of the four gospels, which give the Biographies of Jesus, as preserved in the New Testament. The purpose of the Gospel is stated by John himself, is to show that Jesus of Nazareth was Christ the Son of God and that believers in Him might have eternal life. (Tom Ascol) To be Christ like is not only preaching the gospel, or singing about it: it must be to live a Christian life that to be as disciples of Jesus Christ See what happened to the disciples of Jesus Christ after they had travelled with Him for three years, even their accent was like that of Jesus Christ. That means following every step that Jesus had. Sometimes we do not take these things seriously. To be like Him means that everything He did we must do also if we want to be like Him, that means everything He did we must do, where He sacrificed His life for us we must do also we must sacrifice our lives for others. Originally, the goal of every Christian is to be like Christ. Sometimes in our life's journey, we get carried away and loose the central aim. (Romans 8:28) (KJV) we must put all our effort in trying to be like Christ. If we are like Him, that means our lives will be transformed. In all what we do, we must ask Him to intervene because this world is a sinning world; it is working against us being like Christ. The Lord is so faithful to us that He is working against those forces for our good. The Holy Spirit is always there to protect those who follow Jesus' footsteps and lead them into the right way. So every persecution the Christians suffer, they know that their Saviour also suffered.

THE BOOK OF REVELATIONS IS A FOREWARNING THAT THERE IS DEFINITELY A SECOND COMING:

This book was written so as to forewarn the people that there is definitely a second coming of Christ, so the chosen ones must start running away from the judgement day. Calling on the chosen ones to commit them and live a righteous life now in readiness for that day. What this book is all about is to give its reader a revelation of what is to come. Warning us that these things will definitely come to pass and that judgement day will approach as revealed. We are being given what we should expect to see on that day. The purpose is to reveal the fullness of Christ at the same time warning believers and giving them hope in their journey of life. Let us ask the Lord to give us understanding We can read and read, but if it is not revealed to us, we cannot understand it.(John the Elder/pbs.org.evelations) The book of Revelation was written sometime around 96 AD in Asia Minor. The author was probably a Christian from Ephesus known as "John the Elder" according to the book, this John was on the island of Patmos, not far from the cost of Asia Minor, "because of the word of God and the testimony of Jesus" (Revelation 1:10) (KJV).

CHAPTER 7

MULTICULTURALISM IS SEEN AS A CONTROVERSIAL ISSUE:

As technology develops, it has caused so many people to migrate to seeking for education and some knowledge that might be found in those countries. This has also caused some people to be hired by other countries because of their knowledge. This has seen cultures mixing with other cultures sometimes, although people are mixing because of economical situations, sometimes you find that people do not forget their roots. As people of different races are mixing, there have also been a lot of inter-marriages. That system of intermarriage cannot be seen to be changing in the near future. Although technology is developing and making things easier, but multiculturalism has not made them any easy. Where technology is developing, it is making things easier and better, whereas multiculturalism has not made them any better.

MULTI-CULTURALISM HAS BECOME A CONFLICTING ISSUE, IN THE LAST DECADE OF THE TWENTIETH CENTURY:

What has made multiculturalism a conflicting issue is that the different cultures have their own values in their own cultures. It appears some of these cultures do not want to compromise. The things of this world are very attractive that we have to be always alert. The value aspect has made adapting very difficult because no one wants to let go their values. Although the laws say there must be some equality, but the people themselves tend to discriminate each other. Even in the work settings, some jobs are left for some ethnic groups this is crafted in such a way that it may not be noticed. *Understanding Multi-culturalism:*

Multi-culturalism can be thought of as a reality, when we try to analyse, it is something that is happening and it is in existence, no one is able yet to tell how it came about and how it will end, it emerged in the last half of the twentieth century. As an ideal, it is a controversial view of human society that has become something that someone would always want to look at closely and something that one would like to think again in the last decade of the twentieth century. Some scholars say multiculturalism emerged in the last half of the twentieth century, while some scholars say, it should have been specified how, because multiculturalism has been there since the Persian times or the Samaritan times. The problem that is arising between multiculturalism and Christianity is that it has become a three way activity, because politics has also come into play. So many countries in the world have become multicultural; it is in these cultures that there are some religions that are completely against Christianity in such a way that they never moved an inch towards Christianity. Politics has said, because they are accommodating every culture, they have their rights not to hear anything about Christianity, yet Christianity is asked to compromise. Here multiculturalism has not done what was done by Christianity to culture; they selected the good ones in culture and modified the bad ones. But multiculturalism has said leave everything that is in Christianity. With the fact that in the 260s AD, regardless of the persecution that Christianity suffered, Christianity grew while paganism was declining. That did not go very well with the forces that were against Christianity. These forces, if they find any loophole, they take advantage of that and try to wipe Christianity all together. Today's Christians should take an example from those that were persecuted but never gave in. Multiculturalism has taken a new twist, of appearing like they have a valid reason, while their aim is not to give Christianity a chance. They want to ensure that Christianity is wiped off the face of the earth.

HOW MULTI-CULTURALISM IS AFFECTING CHRISTIANITY IN SOCIETY:

Multiculturalism has affected Christianity in that as technology has developed, it has brought together so many different cultures. Some of these cultures do not believe in Christianity, so it becomes difficult to accommodate them. So Christianity is being practised with caution, taking into consideration not to offend other cultures that do not believe in Christianity.

MULTI-CULTURALISM IN THE LAST DECADE OF THE TWENTIETH CENTURY:

CHAPTER 8

DECLINE AND FALL OF THE ROMAN EMPIRE:

(Edward Gibbon) The contributing factor to the fall of the Roman Empire was the rise in Christianity. Christianity had to breathe some fresh air during the time of Constantine the great. He allowed Christianity to be a recognised religion. In 410 CE Visigoth's army invaded the Roman Empire. During the time of Constantine persecution for Christian ended. The other most reason of the cause of the fall was it left its borders too loose that as a result in was infiltrated by barbarian tribes such as Goths invaded the Roman Empire that was in 410 AD.

BYZANTIUM:

Byzantium was the Eastern part of the Roman Empire. The capital was Constantinople (present Istanbul), the fall of Byzantium was in 1453.The army stormed into Constantinople on May 29 1453 the inversion led by Mehmed mostly converted the city into mosque.

PACIFISM:

Pacifism in Christianity means that any form of violence is not tolerable because violence does not go well with Christian belief, because they take their example from Christ Himself going to the cross like a sheep to the slaughter. Christ is looking at His followers to do the same and follow His footsteps. That is the reason why it becomes different to the earthly kingdom where they use violence to solve their disputes. This book pleads with its reader to emulate and follow the example and put it into practice for it pay dividends in the end. Sometimes Christians are at loggerheads with non-Christians, because sometimes when the kingdom of this world is at war they want Christians to be also involved. Christians say they are following the footsteps of their Saviour.

Pacifism is the decline of violence in Christianity, emulating Jesus Christ.

CHAPTER 9

TODAY'S CHRISTIANS APPEAR TO BE COMPROMISING THEIR CHRISTIANITY:

When one is compromising Christianity, means someone might not be truly a Christian or truly culturalism. There are so many Christians today who are doing it; the Lord will not recognise such Christians. Revelations chapter 2 reminds us that we are in the world of sin, so we must try to guard against all the temptations that come to us. Sometimes we fall in a trap of wanting to be identified as church goers without truly being in spirit and in truth. Let us not deceive ourselves for the Lord sees everything and He records everything. Do not lose your first love to God.

THE ROLE CHRISTIANITY PLAY IN EDUCATING PEOPLE:

(The Role of Christianity in Civilisation) Christianity should be taking its example from Christ Himself because Christ as a Messiah, His Mission on earth was mainly Preaching and teaching. As Christians are taking it from Him, that is the reason why in the medieval times Christianity started many schools. Unlike today when most governments have taken over, many schools were missionary schools. Although the governments have taken over most of the educational institutions, missionary schools still exist. Some missionary schools are still providing education as up to the university level. Missionary schools used to provide Christian education as well. But since multiculturalism has taken centre stage, the governments are saying to teach Christian education in schools might offend some religions which are not Christian in origin. It started looking like those who never liked Christianity were winning, but as Jesus said to Peter that on you I will build my church. It appears Jesus Himself Defends His church, there were times like times of Christian persecution when defending Christianity was very grievous in that many people were martyr trying to defend Christianity, but still Christianity survived. Christ will always give His people courage to become tactful and courageous to soldier on. Also Christianity was very much concerned with the health of the people, in that many hospitals were mission hospitals. So, it can be said with certainty that Christianity is a major source of social services which means Christianity is very much concerned with the welfare of the people. Contrary to what could be argued that Christianity kills culture, it would not kill culture when it has the welfare of the people at heart, instead it could sometimes it is seen to be promoting art and culture, only that when it does it, it is done in such a way that it does not promote primitively but to promote civilisation which everyone is striving for civilisation.

Festivals such as Easter and Christmas seem to dominate most of the Western World calendar. It could be argued that Christianity is indulging in politics too much unlike an example which was given by Jesus Himself who kept on refusing to be drawn into politics. The reason why Christianity seem to be very much in politics could be that it is trying to protect human rights which is very much part of Christianity. Take for example slavery could Christianity stand by while human beings created in the image of God were being treated as the property of the slave owner.

Culture has sometimes promoted polygamy, female infanticide treating women as second class citizens. There is some debate still going on even to this date of whether women should be ordained? There is now a division Among Christians themselves. Some denominations are already ordaining women, while some are still saying Jesus had male disciples only. As the Spirit leads the church, they will come to an agreement one day. Like today, Jesus taught the story of the good Samaritan which very much teaches human rights today., Jesus was saying there is no gentile or Jew but we are all the sons and daughters of one Father, which multiculturalism is all about, which today might be taken wrongly and becomes a hindrance to Christianity yet Jesus never meant it that way. Christianity has condemned marital infidelity, it has not entertained divorce or to have multiple wives. Christianity has taught that it is not good to have so many children which you would not be able to give enough support. Culturally baby girls were not liked that in some cases were killed which Christianity said it was anti-God or antichristian. In today's modern world, women have played a very important role Christianity and worldly affairs and have shown not being different from men. Women have taken a lead in science and technology Theology health and industry in general they shown their ability in all these fields that is the reason why modern society is moving away from any form of segregation.

CHRISTIANS SHOULD FAITHFULLY AND GENTLY TRANSFORM SOCIETY:

The business of the churches is to educate the people. This is done to try to alleviate human suffering. Although churches wanted to live luxurious lives, they cannot do that while the people were suffering. It is not enough to give them food and clothing, without educating them; education is important in that when people are educated, they are able to fend for themselves. This is done in obedience to Jesus' new commandment to love one another. According to Paul Copan's article, it appears like Christians are worried why people are not taking heed, yet it is for Christians to take their example from Christ. Christians are not asked for anything but for dedication. If Christians would put some dedication into it, it bears fruit in the end. There is a call for Christians to be a role model, knowing that the Saviour has already set the pace. We have very live examples, currently, of some cultures that are showing some very backwardness, examples are Hindu cultures. It may be argued that why singling them out for mention, but if looked at very closely, it appears very primitive. "Good Faith" by David Kinnaman, urges Christians to take the great commission very seriously. It says that because there are some hidden forces that are trying to snatch away whatever was built by Christianity. It is not encouraged to criticise others and their cultures, without you setting an example; like what Jesus said in (John 4:35), Jesus was very clear that the harvest is ready. What are we waiting for? Let Christians show their good works for the world to be healed. Where ever you are there are people waiting to hear the word, we have no excuse, let us spread the word this is the time we have got. (Judith A. Merkle) "Being Faithful" A Christian of today is faced with so many big challenges: these require a Christian to be more faithful than ever before. Since a Christian is not separated from the world that means a Christian is facing the changes that are happening in society and its cultures. Since the world is modernising, that is, the mixing of cultures and becoming multi-cultural. The multi-culturalism has come about as a result of society becoming technical, and becoming more industrialised. So Christianity suffers because some cultures are not Christian, hence they say leave Christianity and let us be multicultural. Since culture has been defined as a way of life, it is now trying to dilute Christianity. That is why a Christian is being advised to wear an armoury of faith, filled with the Holy Spirit, which are the only tools a Christian has at their disposal. We are to continue living in the society as per Jesus' commandment that Christians are the salt of the earth. When salt is used in the food, it does not stay outside the food, but mixes fully with the food in order for it to taste like it has salt. We are asked to mix with society, but at the same time keeping our saltiness.

THE INFLUENCE OF CHRISTIANITY ON HUMAN NATURE:

Christianity has also in a clear way, some influence on those who claim to be philosophers and also has influence on politicians. It has been found that if they (Christians) are involved fully in politics, the end result will be that they will be corrupted. Christianity must take their example from Jesus, who was at a time when the Jews were under the colonial rule of the Romans. The Jews thought that as powerful as Jesus was, He was going to liberate them from the yoke of the Romans and set them free.

Jesus never entertained their thoughts. They mistook His kingship with the earthly kingdom. As Christians it may be that they are also getting carried away if they start mixing the two kingdoms. An advice to those who would like to follow Christianity is that they have to ask for generous providence to be able to separate the two kingdoms.

There is always a temptation when the two kingdoms meet, to separate them becomes difficult yet they are two separate kingdoms. The other one is a physical kingdom, while the other is a Spiritual kingdom. Those who decide to follow the Christian kingdom must know that they follow it in truth and in Spirit. The difference with these two is that the earthly kingdom rules over, yet the heavenly kingdom rules under. The other two differences with these two kingdoms is that, when they want change, the earthly kingdom wants to see the change there and then, if the change does not happen, then it resorts to using force, yet with the heavenly kingdom any change is planned well in advance.

CHAPTER 10

THE WORK OF THE CHURCH IS TO GIVE PEOPLE MORALE AND TO MAKE THEM KEEP THEIR ETHICS:

Christianity believes that it is part of their duty to act in a moral way. This involves helping others around them. The church plays a vital role as it provides a very important role of helping people, and the support that it gives to the destitute people. Learn what the church can provide and how it helps the persecuted in the modern world. Most of the Christian's hours are spent at work, only 2 hour spent at the church, but those two hours should be the hours to launch us into the world. Our places of work should be places of worship. For God is Spirit those who worship Him must worship Him in truth and in Spirit. As He is Spirit that means He is everywhere with us, it is good for us because we can worship Him where ever we are and whatever we are doing, we must be connected.

THE WORK OF THE CHURCH IS TO REPRESENT THE HEAVENLY KINGDOM ON EARTH:

The work of the church whether it is a group or individual it has to be a representative of the heavenly kingdom. That is it must be seen to have the welfare of the people at heart. Individually or as a group they must be able to sacrifice their lives for others as an example given by Jesus Himself, which shows He had people at heart. The way the church or individual should behave is all in the Bible. The Bible guides us according to the wishes of God because all scripture were inspired by God for guiding us in our life's journey. (Matthew 5:44) (KJV) By saying "love your enemies" Jesus is asking us to follow His example, Jesus says, we must follow His example because He came to earth to be exemplary in everything, as He himself is like His Father. The Father makes rain to rain on those who do not care about Him. He makes the son to shine on every one even those who do not even know Him. But should not make us go on sinning because His mercy is in abundance, because there will be a time of judgement, Jesus Himself loved His enemies. He gave Peter a curse when he wanted to revenge on Jesus' enemies who were arresting Him, Jesus said to Peter, it is never done like that, whoever uses a sword will die of a sword. (Matthew 26:52) (KJV) Sometimes by so thinking that we are defending ourselves, we are preventing the will of God to be done in earth as it is in heaven, if at all Peter had succeeded in preventing Jesus's arrest, Jesus would not have died and the will of God would not have been done on earth. Jesus had perfect commitment to His Father's will; let us know it from now that the kingdom of God is never advanced with swords, but with faith and obedience, "Amen". Let every Christian bear in mind that when Jesus was on earth, he was establishing the heavenly kingdom, and if we follow his example, we will become citizens of the heavenly kingdom. The devil is trying with all his power of darkness for that kingdom not to be established on earth, if we look back to the days of the apostles after the Pentecost, most of the values have been lost somewhere along the line, we are to ask God to have mercy on us and intervene Himself to save us, reform us and give us the authority to deal with those evil spirits.

The non-Christians say, "Do not take the law into your own hands" which means they know Christianity even though they do not want to come into the open. On the other hand, when we love our enemies we are creating new relationships. We have to strive and ask for divine revelation when we interpret the scriptures, ask for His guidance for the scriptures were inspired by Him, by asking Him we can have the real meaning of God's laws. Sometimes we get carried away and mix the two kingdoms, the earthly kingdom and the heavenly kingdom.

In (Luke chapter 10) (KJV), when they were trying to trap Jesus, He even gave them the example of the Good Samaritan. There was a great enmity between Jews and the Samaritans. When a certain man met with the robbers, was left for dead. The two men who were related to him, passed by, yet he was picked up by The Good Samaritan who was said to be an enemy to him. This teaches us clearly that the heavenly kingdom has no enemies. The one who was said to be enemy number one is the one who was savour to the victim of the robbers. Let the heavenly kingdom come on earth now.

(Matthew 5:5) (KJV) "The meek shall inherit the earth" Why did Jesus seem to mix the earthly kingdom with the heavenly kingdom, when He said the meek shall inherit the earth, instead of inheriting the heavenly kingdom? Jesus meant that His disciples should be exemplary. If they showed meekness, the earthly people shall see the goodness in that and that would mean the heavenly kingdom is being practised on earth, hence, the heavenly kingdom would have come on earth, then the Father would be glorified. Jesus is asking us to live such a life here on earth so that people will see our good works. When we practise meekness, people seem to take advantage of that, but then Jesus says the heavenly kingdom is made of such people and the glory of the Lord will be seen. Being meek means waiting patiently for the Lord, when it looks like those not waiting are getting better quickly than those waiting. Being meek means trusting in the Lord, and gives Him His place as the one who holds everything in His hand. Even before that He used to say that I will fight your battles for you. Lest you think that you have done it with your own power. Humble yourself before the Lord and put all your trust in Him for He is worth that, and will not let us down, but to do it for us.

MAN RESEMBLES GOD BECAUSE GOD SAID, "LET US MAKE MAN IN OUR IMAGE":

The Lord said, "Let us make man in our own image", that was on the last day of creation, (Genesis 1:26) (KJV).By saying let us make man in our own image, that means He loves man. He loves a man because He breathed His Spirit into a man. This means a man has both flesh and spirit/soul. With the fact that man was made in the image "likeness" of God means that a man has to behave like the one he is likened unto. If a man does not behave like he is supposed to behave, he is betraying that responsibility. (John 4:24) (KJV) says "God is Spirit", but man is made of both flesh and spirit, Adam was made of flesh, but God breathed His Spirit into him. Originally he was supposed not to die until sin came in through the lies of the devil. Since a man is said to be created in the likeness of God that means a man is created differently from all other creation. This means a man has the ability to think unlike other creations. That is the reason why a man has got to have dominion over everything on earth, (Genesis 1:28) (KJV), So a man should behave in a manner that shows some responsibility. A man should try to preserve the life of everything that is on earth. In other words, it means everything on earth is looking at a man as their saviour, the responsibility which should not be betrayed. As a man was created in the image of God, so a man must represent the heavenly kingdom here on earth.

"Morally a man is created in righteousness and perfect innocence, a reflection of God's holiness". That is the reason why when God looked at it, He said "it was good", (Genesis 1:31) (KJV). If anything, man should strive to maintain that originality. The reason why laws are there comes from evil, because originally the law was not there. Laws are trying to take a man to the original state but in a harsh way.

"Socially humanity is created for fellowship; this reflects God's triune and His love of man. God had a good relationship with Adam and Eve in the Garden of Eden until the devil intervened into their fellowship. So that broken fellowship was passed on to their dependence. That means a man is trying to mend that broken relationship. Adam and Eve had a free choice, but they chose to use that free choice to rebel against their Creator, this choice was handed down to us. How are we using this free choice? This is where we should ask for divine intervention and that promised Holy Spirit to fill us so that we can be filled and guided during the journey of our life. We have all the freedom to make a choice, which is the reason why all things concerning Christianity are not compulsory. We still have that freedom to make a choice, but in the end, we are hanging ourselves. Watch out, every day we are seeing the effects of sin everywhere around us. Even though we had fallen into that original sin, God loves His creation, in that He decided to give a man a second chance in which He expects us not to abuse that second chance again.

TO WORSHIP IS TO MAKE A SACRIFICE:

Worship is giving honour to God in various ways, giving what you have or doing something, we must always ask God to transform us so that we can be able to worship Him in truth and in Spirit. Without Him intervening, we will not be able to do it. True worship should worship with sacrifice, for worship to be of value, it has to be sacrificial, in your social service. The Christians who were before us, sacrificed their lives in order to preserve Christianity. To sacrifice is slaughtering an animal or a person. Surrender something that you possess as an offering to God. Offer your time, your possession or your strength to others for the promotion of the work of God. Christ offered Himself on the cross for you and me. Worship without sacrifice is one of the seven sins. Think how close you become with relatives that are the closeness you should be with your God. Be very close to Him such that you will not want to see His name being tarnished. Or that you would not want to see anyone created in His image being treated inhumanly. To worship with a sacrifice is to have a desire to do exactly as He Himself did, He sacrificed His blood for us, are we able to sacrifice our wealth or our strength in order for all the glory to be to Him. Let us strive to and let us help us to be able to worship Him in truth and in spirit and in truth. Sometimes in life things will appear to be very tough, going so we seem to choose the easy one to do. new very good example4s to follow, the Old or the New Testaments they are all full of people who sacrificed, like Abraham in the Old Testament, also the New Testament Jesus Himself was a sacrificial lamb, and sat an example for His followers . The apostles suffered a lot for us to be like we are today.

CHAPTER 11

SACRED CHRIST AND SACRED SCRIPTURE:

Since God inspired scriptures to be written, He has to ensure they are sacred so scripture have to be treated with the sacred they deserve. To follow these scripture will lead to worshiping the true God. Through the scripture is the way God reveals Himself to man, hence the church people who follow these scriptures must lead a pure life. Jesus had to take human flesh so that He could be understood. Otherwise if He had come as a heavenly being He would not have been understood. He has inspired the writing of the scripture; He reveals His ways and Himself in the scriptures to those who seek Him diligently. Those who through those scriptures will have faith in Him, He will build a wall of righteousness around them that His people are protected. When Jesus speaks of us being born again He means we must be born spiritually as in John 3:5, this means pure repentance and committing Jesus to your heart: after you have done your part of committing yourself to him the Lord will make changes in your life which is not the change from human being but real divine change transformation. There is a combination that there is a hidden remission of sins in His baptism and also the washing away of sins in His blood. There is a danger of not believing in His baptism as this is betraying the will of God and forsaking His salvation. Strive to strengthen your faith in God, through believing in the baptism. The Bible is the book of the law of God, which means, like any other laws, cannot be changed just to suit an individual. The scripture, since it is inspired by Him it has survived the test of time, unlike any other history books, it has served many generations, and has a potential to serve many generations to come.

HUMAN NATURE IS TO DO THE WILL OF GOD:

A human being is made in such a way that one will be found to behave in the same manner as the other, which means what one does the other will have to follow without a command, and some of the deeds of a human being will just happen. Try to follow the nature of a human being they will differ from those of other creations, skilful, scientific, communicable and behaving humanly. Human nature is the human's characteristics which are his way of thinking and his feelings and how he acts, which seem to happen naturally. The cause of these natural characteristics which are psychologically and neuroscientific ally is not known. The culture and also how a person is brought up sometimes shows human nature. Economics, ethics, politics and theology all seem to build human nature. When they always happen they become the norms of human nature. Since there is a combination of so many things the research still continues to find out exactly how human nature is. Human nature is also referred to as human behaviour, this refers to whether it is good or bad, selfish or aggressive, but by trying to get the good out of it human behaviour might change by pursuing to resolve human behaviour and transform it. Can happiness be measured? Sometimes a plus can hide a minus, and also something gained may cancel something lost. The nature of human being must be distinctive from that of animals and the rest of creation. A human being should show to be above all creation, human nature reflects God's attributes, and we love taking examples from Him. That means we have to be compassionate, faithful, kind, patient and just, but sometimes sin wants to separate us from all that.

THE RESURRECTION OF THE DEAD:

"The Bible teaches that when Christ returns, the Kingdom of God will be established on earth". The Bible is silent of the dead going to heaven immediately after death. In (Acts 2:29, 34) (KJV), Peter told the people at Pentecost that when David died and was buried long ago he was still in his grave waiting for the second coming of Jesus. (John 3:13) (KJV) confirms it by saying that "No man has ascended to heaven but he who came down from heaven".

The dead saints of Old and New Testament are still sleeping in their graves, awaiting resurrection. Many verses refer to the dead as "sleeping". In (1 Corinthians 15) (KJV) Even though Jesus after His resurrection, He stayed 40 days to prove that He resurrected from the dead, still people without faith are still doubting. But here Paul tells us of the resurrection of Jesus as a model of the resurrection of the dead. That is the time when the mortal will be transformed into immortal. So the Bible clearly states that the kingdom of God will be established on earth when everything will be transformed, and this will be an everlasting kingdom. (Matthew 6:9-13) (KJV) tells us to ask from the Father who loves and very prepared to listen to us, for His kingdom, that is, His Spiritual reign to come on earth and everything and everything on earth to resemble what is in heaven. When we say, thy will be done on earth, we are giving all the glory to Him how will this kingdom come? (1 Timothy 6:15) (KJV) states that He has got power more than any other king who ever established their kingdoms here on earth

THE RELATIONSHIP THE BIBLICAL WORLD VIEW HAS WITH CHRISTIANITY OR GOD:

The Bible was written by 40 different writers who lived at different times. These writers never set together to formulate a plan on how to go about it. This shows how God inspired them to write the Scriptures, as found in (2 Timothy 3: 16) (KJV), because He loves the world and He wants it saved, that is the reason why He inspired them to write these Scriptures and also gave His only Son as in (John 3:16) (KJV), so it is out of love for the world, that He inspired these people to write scriptures. By doing all this He wants there to be peace in the world, to have peace in the world is when we love one another, like He has shown us, and He has given us an example which we must follow. He gave these instructions in (John 14:27) (KJV), when we have peace, we will live life to its fullest like in (John 10:10) (KJV), life itself is surely a battle; the Christian must always fight this battle, which must be won. Christians are always surrounded by choices between culture and Christianity. They may disagree with some aspects of it, but always think of culture as an ally rather than a threat. They can interact comfortably and uncritically with the reigning social, cultural and political trends of the day. There is a dominant culture which they incorporate easily into their lives and churches. These Christians and their churches tend to change colours like chameleons as the culture context changes. They take culture as something ordained by God. So they view it and find there is nothing bad in it. It is sometimes forgotten that sometimes culture is tainted by sin, and hence sometimes loses its direction.

THE RELATIONSHIP BETWEEN GOD AND MAN IS ON LOVE:

(godonthe.net) (accessed 18.8.2020) (Genesis 1:26) (KJV), Then God said, "let us make man in our image in our likeness, and let them rule over the fish of the sea and the birds of the air, over the livestock, over all the earth and over the entire creature that move along the ground". (csmonitor.com) (accessed 18.8.2020) it appears unwise for a man to try to separate from God, because before man even asked for it, he was made in the image of God, and was given dominion on earth, Instead of showing some responsibility, man abuses that responsibility. What a man has to be reminded of is that although he was made from dust, God breathed His spirit into a man hence the man carries the likeness of God. The problem arises, because the man was given freedom of choice. The man abused that freedom of choice and chose to rebel against the Creator. Sometimes we abuse that freedom of choice and start behaving like we are at par with the Creator. Sometimes we forget our relationship and there is no communication with the one we were created in whose image. Sometimes if a man has rebelled against the Creator, it becomes difficult to come back, because coming back means repentance. Yet He is always saying there is room for reconciliation. When we were groping our way not knowing where to go or what to do, Jesus showed us the way. When He said it was finished, he was saying, He had accomplished His mission on earth. However, He was going, He was going to send us the comforter, who would dwell with us for ever. Our relationship is like this, He loved us, created us in His likeness, gave us dominion over all the earth, in return we have to give Him all the glory, come to Him with all the praises and revere Him because He is sovereign. If we do that, we keep our relationship preserved that way. We have to keep our relationship by talking to Him all the time, not to wait until there is a problem, but talking all the time.

THE TRANSITION FROM JUDAISM TO CHRISTIANITY WAS A COMPLEX ISSUE:

The problem arose when the apostles were trying to follow exactly as Jesus had taught, and as he had commanded them to do at the great commission. The Jews thought they were the chosen people, so when someone wanted to introduce something new they said that was misleading the people and they said, that was not what God wanted. They never wanted to adapt to the Jesus way of doing things. So all what they were doing they thought that they were preserving what God wanted. They took those who were following the teachings of Jesus as being against God. That belief that they were the chosen people made them think that they were superior to others. To those who still hold on to Judaism still hold that belief of superiority up to this day. Some followers of Christ had understood that the gentiles had to be included in Christianity. But some Jews resented that, insisting that they were the only chosen people, so the division arose and it became controversial that they had to split

CHAPTER 12

THE JEWS THOUGHT THAT JESUS HAD COME TO UNDO THE LAW OF MOSES, THIS LED TO HIS CRUCIFIXION:

Among the many reasons in our days that led to the crucifixion of Jesus is that Jesus was exceedingly inclusive and kind, He was crucified for welcoming the outcasts. He was murdered for hanging out with prostitutes and half-breeds. He was killed because He courageously loved the poor and sinners that His enemies could not take it any longer. Matthew 26:63-66 (Luke 15:2) It is not enough for the reader to pretend as if really the Messiahship of Jesus, it is complex that we need to ask for grace and mercy, because by our deeds we may be crucifying Him. They grumbled against Jesus for eating with sinners and tax collectors. They killed Him for claiming to be the Son of God and the King of Israel (Matthew 27:39-43) (KJV). Those who were passing by mocked him, saying, you helped many help yourself Even the chief priests joined mocking Him. What they did not that it was God's plan of salvation. By killing Him they thought they silenced Him, without knowing that they had fulfilled God's plan. We have problems when others use divine revelation when others have no revelation at all. The main reason they gave, trying to justify their killing him, was that he calls himself the king of the Jews, and that He calls himself the Son of God. (According to them it was blasphemy) but the most thing is that they never understood him, even to this day he is never understood.

THEY CRUCIFIED JESUS BECAUSE THEY FAILED TO UNDERSTAND HIS MESSIAHSHIP:

Jesus was bringing an inward transformation, That is, what he was teaching was really from God, like what Nicodimus found out, yet he was in a group of those opposing Jesus, whenever you are doing good, stick to the goodness people will notice the goodness. To get salvation we need to really transform and humble ourselves before the Lord, for His grace alone can save us, no matter how rich you might be, no richness can buy salvation.(Romans 1:16) Jesus is the intercessor between our sins and God. Sometimes good things are not readily seen, we have to ask for God's grace to help us to understand the goodness that is in His love that He gives His own Son like in John 3:16, now it is up to us to accept such love in order to get salvation. To follow Jesus is to side with those who are looked down upon, this means standing with the forgotten, the abused and those who are socially forgotten, that means that we are following the footsteps of our Saviour. We tend to find it easy to say, when He says it is not easy, because when it is the real situation, we do not stand, to defend our promise of dying for our friends like Jesus did. Loving Jesus with real love is very costly, because if we are following His footsteps we should do exactly as he did it, it cost Him His blood, it cost Him His life.

JESUS CHRIST THE REAL STORY.

According to the Jewish culture, and belief, there is only one God. For someone to come and start claiming that he was the son of God, to them it was blasphemy. For to try to convince them that he was the awaited Messiah, could not make sense to them because they had already ruled him out because he had called himself the son of God.

What they thought they had succeeded in was to silence him by putting him to death. Jesus was hated from three angles: from Judaism, paganism, and from the Roman Government who felt threatened by him thinking that his kingdom was a political kingdom. The confusion has spilt into this present day. It requires divine revelation to be able to differentiate between the earthly kingdom and the heavenly kingdom. The confusion that can be seen currently originated from the crucifixion. Jesus did not offer resistance when He was led to the cross because He came here to earth on a mission. If He had resisted, His mission would have been defeated. This book reminds the reader to set goals and to be on a mission; as a result, you may get to a stage where you will not resist the cross when it comes in your life. When the cross comes in your life you will be prepared to take up your cross like Jesus did. We are being reminded that as we are travelling the journey of life it is preparing us for that cross. Following Jesus requires loving the people, because that is what He Himself did and He left the mission to us to accomplish. We must always be working for the good of the poor and proclaim good news for the poor, that was the reason why Jesus had to be led to the cross without offering any resistance.

JESUS DID NOT OFFER ANY RESISTANCE AS HE WAS LED TO THE CROSS:

If Jesus had offered resistance as He was led to the cross, His mission on earth would not have been accomplished. Jesus was submitting to the will of the Father the will of the Father was for the salvation of the people. The Holy Spirit now applies the work of redemption to Jesus' followers. When Jesus was led to the cross, it was the climax of God's redemptive plan. Man's freedom is in the cross where all what happened to Adam was reversed. That is why it is always advisable for Christians to always look to the cross for salvation because that is where we were saved, because sin was conquered.

JESUS' POWERS WERE NOT SHOWN ON THE CROSS BUT AT THE RESURRECTION:

When Jesus was led to the cross without offering any resistance, it did not mean that He had no power. God does His things according to plan, when He plans He wants things to happen according to plan. We must give all the glory to him knowing that even this present day He had made a plan for it. We have to ask for His grace and mercy to give us a revelation to see His love around us every day. If we focus on the resurrection, we will see that it was done for us so that we get salvation; we have to be faithful to be able to see this revelation. If people were now in doubt that was now answered at the resurrection when all the plans of the devil were proved wrong. This proved that the power of darkness could not overcome the power of the light. That power at resurrection was given to us at Pentecost.

WHO WAS JESUS CHRIST OF NAZARETH?

Jesus of Nazareth came into the world to set an example; His purpose was to save the world. His message was;"Repent for the kingdom of heaven is at hand". Is that message received at all, if it is received are people abiding by it. People are still visiting Nazareth where Jesus grew up; they want to have first-hand information. Many Christians today are making pilgrimage to visit this place, Nazareth is known today as the Arab capital of Israel.

JESUS WAS GOD IN THE FLESH:

"Jesus is God in man "incarnate" meaning that, He is the spirit came in a visible form as human, it is the belief of the Christians that He was God in human form. He is part of the trinity; Jesus is fully human and fully divine". He did not just come at the time of his birth but that He was there even before the creation. (John 1:1) (KJV) "In the beginning was the Word, and the Word was with God, and the Word was God" Word was God's source of message to the people through the prophets. Verse 14 "And the Word was made flesh, and dwelt among us, (and we beheld His glory, the glory as of only, begotten of the Father,) full of grace and truth". God decided to put us to live here on earth preparing for the next life, which should be eternity, so let us prepare for that. Christ came to give us the fullness of God, which we have to appreciate that God loves us, it is only us who drift away from Him and from His love. Before Christ came People knew God partially, Christ is the perfect expression of God in human form. We should not confuse, He is fully human and fully divine, we ask the Lord to make us commit this to our minds and make it our treasure for life.

JESUS DIED FOR OUR CAUSE:

Discover the story of the greatest man who ever lived. Pray for the revelation of his word. In other words, we are saying God increase our knowledge, two thousand years: the story of Christ is as new as it was before, because it is the story of the past, present, and future. The story is not a fiery fairy or fable. The story of Jesus is surprising that even though he was born of the Spirit, he went through life like any other child in his area. That is the reason why they would not understand him, and went as far as to condemn him to death. Even the present day, it is required to ask for divine revelation to be able to understand his story. The biggest trap we are faced with today is the choice. We have freedom of choice; we tend to abuse that choice, because we have the freedom of choice. Now that the choice is ours, we chose to separate ourselves from Him, yet if we believed in him, we become the children of God. If you choose to follow him, he will give you fresh life and transforms you to be like him. The way to be transformed is when we confess our sins, and surrendering our lives to him. When we pray we are admitting that we are sinners, once you have realised you sinned ask for forgiveness. It is not enough to know that we are sinners and just do nothing about it but confess and ask to cleanse. We are happy that there is someone who loves us, we acknowledge that Jesus died for our sins, and to believe that he died and rose from the dead. We can communicate with him through prayer. All he suffered on the cross was to pay the debt for us because of his love to us. Since Jesus came to earth to set an example, we have to emulate his example. His love goes to the extent of dying for others. If you sincerely invite him to your heart, he is faithful enough he will come into your heart and transform you, his ways are in the Bible.

JESUS CHRIST IS THE ONLY WAY TO GOD, THERE IS NO OTHER WAY:

God loves us and He wants to see us saved, but sometimes we move away from Him. But when we have moved away from Him it requires a lot of courage to come back to Him and say, Lord I had gone astray and I stayed far away from you God. The problem we face sometimes is that we want the Lord to look for us where we are hiding unable to look face to face with

Him. Yet if we realise that we have gone astray, we must have the courage to come back to Him, He is very willing to take us back. The advice for us is to follow the example from Jesus, who lives a perfect life, because He is always in contact with His Father, which means if we are in contact with Jesus, we will be in contact with the Father, as well. The Bible states clearly that if we commit ourselves to Him we will be saved. We must always talk to Him through prayer. Prayer is a way of staying connected to the Father through Jesus Christ. We may say that we are waiting for the second coming of Christ, but are we ready? The reason why we should keep connected through prayer is that we drift away slowly. Even if we read the Bible, we need divine revelation to be able to understand what was inspired in it before for that inspiration to be revealed to us. What happened to Jesus should keep us searching. The Messiah was promised long before, but not promised that He would be born in a manger. We were not promised that it would take thirty years growing like an ordinary child in the area where He grew up. When He was growing, did they know that He was the Messiah? Some great things might be happening among us today, but we might not be taking any note of it at all, this requires divine revelation.

CHAPTER 13

CHRISTIANITY STARTED (MOSTLY BY HIS DISCIPLES WHO WERE JEWS AND OF A JEWISH CULTURE) AFTER JESUS HAD ASCENDED:

Jesus was born in a Jewish home, lived in a Jewish culture; He did not reform or transform Judaism. Jesus was of a divine nature and of human nature; it requires divine revelation on our part to be able to understand His two natures. We should not try to confine him to one particular nature, we should be able to accept his uniqueness and move forward with the reality as it is. The uniqueness comes in that he himself came here for every human creation. When he was speaking to the Jews he said he had not come to do away with the law, but to confirm their culture, this they did not understand, which shows that there is required some divine revelation to enable us to understand the relationship that exist between culture and Christianity. These are very encouraging words to every reader of this book to understand that no one would say their culture has been killed. Otherwise this is depending on how it is put across. Jesus is here revealing the salvation plan as it was planned at creation; Jesus is here giving a divine revelation of His mission on earth, which was to fulfil the salvation plan. We are advised to ask for the Holy Spirit which should transform us to join the trinity.

Jesus kept on emphasising his relation with God; he kept on telling us that if the Holy Spirit is on us, we shall be like him who is like his Father.

The transition from Judaism to Christianity did not come about easily, simply or quickly. It was a complex process which took one hundred years, starting from the crucifixion of Jesus, and which had different causes and effects depending on whether it is looked at from a point of view of Judaism or Christianity. Also the question of legal status as seen through Roman eyes also has some relationship to this issue.

That is the reason why it is said that Christianity did not come easily or quickly because for them to change from Judaism to Christianity was not that simple because, that meant relinquishing what they called their culture to Christianity, which they thought Jesus was trying to make them abandon their culture, yet Jesus was quite clear on that when he said that he had not come to do away with the law, but to fulfil it. This they did not quite get at first, because this kind of saying required an inspiration from above to understand what Jesus meant.

It appears this is currently affecting us to this present day, where we fall into the same trap as the Jews. The Jews thought the gentiles were the unchosen people, but the gentiles received the Holy Spirit without going through the Jewish culture.

Those Jews who converted to Christianity found themselves caught in between, wanting to adopt the Christian faith and wanting to adhere to their culture. This has set a pace for our life application. It appears today's Christian is falling into that temptation which befell those early Jews.

The term "Jewish Christian" appears in historical texts contrasting Christians of Jewish origin. Some of the reasons why they would not believe in him are that they lost focus on the Messiahship. The Jews thought that their culture was the only culture that should be followed, made them to be unpopular among the gentiles.

WAS JESUS AT FAULT THAT LED TO HIM TO BE CRUCIFIED?

(history.com/.amp/news/why-Pontius-palate-executed-jesus) Updated: 16 April 2019/Original: March 6. 2019) Accessed 161 March 2020) we seem to be blinded with earthly riches that we forget about eternal life. Instead Pontius Pilate would have asked Jesus for salvation, instead of him asking

Jesus a question, "What is the truth" It was he himself who was corrupt, Pontius Pilate's life was full of bribery and corruption, and was himself not fit to put Jesus on trial. The reason for Jesus' crucifixion was for you and me. He died for the faults which were not His faults but ours. They were trying to find some faults with Him but the fact still remains that He came here as intercessor between God and our sins. Jesus suffered that great pain in order to restore the relationship between us and God that was torn by sin. By our sin we had drifted away from the presence of God. Even Pontius Pilate did not find fault with Jesus, because the entire fault was being framed, they did not have anything concrete to put against Him. Now that Jesus was crucified they are now beginning to have a blame game. The Jews are saying because they were under the Roman colonial rule hence all the blame should be on the Romans, but when Pilate had said he had found no fault with Him they shouted all the loud to say crucify Him and let His blood be on us and our children, but today they are crying foul. Pilate on his part as he had found no fault on Him, he should have stuck to his words, like he did when they said him that do not write "Jesus of Nazareth King of the Jews" he refused to change it. Now they are all to blame because they all had a hand in His death, if we want to be blameless, we should keep clean. Today we are falling into the same trap of having a blame game, trying to clarify ourselves from being blamed for the death of Christ, instead of repenting and to be remorseful we want to say we are not guilty. There is no running away from it, by our deeds we are leading Him to the cross daily, and we are nailing Him to the cross, let us repent.

THE JEWS DID NOT UNDERSTAND THE MESSIAHSHIP OF JESUS CHRIST:

Judaism's idea of the Messiah differs substantially from the Christian idea of the Messiah. Among the followers of Judaism Jesus is viewed as having been the most influential and the most damaging of all false Messiahs. The traditional belief among the Jews is that the Messiah has not yet come. Relationship with God and us was restored and rein righteousness for all humanity. The idea developed among the Jews, especially those who believed in Isaiah 9. As the description was, their expectations focused on the kingly future of the house of David who would be born in Bethlehem, he would prepare for the coming of the real one. That was the belief of the Jews that the real Messiah was still to come, not Jesus. Yet Christians believe that Jesus is the Messiah, some Jews believe in him only as a Jewish teacher.

Jesus himself did not start the Christian movement, but only that Christianity started after Jesus had long gone. Maybe some of the Jews who could not believe in him were basing their belief on some scrolls discovered in the Dead Sea which said there were going to be two messiahs. They expected Jesus would restore the glory of their kingdom of David, but when that did not happen, they lost all those expectations, and lost all the confidence in him. That is why they are still expecting that the Messiah is still to come. There is a division among the Jews, some believe in Jesus Christ and are Christians, while some still keep their culture of Judaism. Even in the present day Christianity, it requires one to pre-empty yourself so that everything might be revealed to you.

THE ATTITUDE OF THE JEWS TO THE EARLY CHURCH WAS ANTI-CHRISTIAN:

The early Christians expected suffering; Christ had died on the cross, so there was no higher honour than to imitate that death through accepting martyrdom. (1 Peter (4:16) (KJV) expresses it as: "If you suffer as a Christian, do not be ashamed, but praise God that you bear that witness for Christ.

How is it that the church went under such sacrifice? The Roman governor Bithynia of the Black Sea region could not hastate to send for execution those accused of being Christians: the name alone was sufficient death warrant. Reasons for persecution emerged from the record of Christianity's first three centuries. Although the Romans joined in, the persecution was started by the Jews. (2Kinggs 17:29) (KJV). Christianity went through hardship of being persecuted for three hundred years. The Jews never liked them because they took Christianity as a heresy. That means they were suffering from two fronts, because the Roman government thought it would one day revolt against the government. For those years

Christians never gave up until in the end Christianity was recognised as an official religion. The Christians expected suffering because Christ Himself went through that as well. So when they suffered persecution they were happy that they were following the footsteps of their Saviour. Even though Christianity today is no more being killed, but they are suffering psychological persecution. Sometimes the problem that we face is that when change comes we do not want to change just for the sake of not changing. That is the problem that was faced by the early Jews they had grown up during the law of Moses they were in it in such a way that they never thought no one other than that law of Moses could bring them salvation . That is the reason why there was some resistance when Christians were trying to convince them that Christ would bring salvation. The Jews believe in the oneness of God, but Christians say there a trinity this kind of thinking between the two seems to be dragging on until this present day. The Jews cannot be convinced that God can be in human form. The most reason why Christians were persecuted is that they refused to worship the gods of the Romans when they knew very well that there was a living God. The only advice to be given to today's Christians is that they should not be half hearted when coming to the Lord. Today's Christians believe that they should be going along with the two following God and carrying their culture along with them; we need guidance in order to be able to follow a clear path.

PHARISEES AND SADDUCEES WERE PRESERVERS OF CULTURE:

It is important to note that the Sadducees and the Levite Priests were not completely synonymous. Not all Levites, Priests, High Priests and Aristocrats were Sadducees. Some were Pharisees, and many were not members of any group at all. It is widely believed that the Sadducees sought to preserve this priestly line and the authority of the Temple.

When reading the Bible it has to be noted or it must be kept in mind that those books we read now were written 1000s of years ago in different culture than our own, Jesus arrived on the scene during a time of great confusion in religious and political turmoil. Some 700 years before Christ, the northern part (Hebrew Nation) was conquered and integrated into their culture by the Assyrians (721BC), then the Southern part fell to (Babylon) (Persia) in (586BC) then all of it the (Greek Empire) in 331. In 166BC the Maccabean revolt occurred and the Jews took back their sovereignty for about 100 years. Around 61BC Judea along with all of the Greek Empire was conquered by (Rome).

Rome would not allow Jews to establish their kingdom monarchy, but did allow them to rebuild their Temple and worship their own God. Within that religion they were allowed to form some sort of government with some sort of rule on the religious side of the people. This kept the peace at least on the surface so that most of Judea would accept Roman Rule as long as they would keep their religious roots and methods of worship.

Because of wars that were fought, (fighting for the earthly kingdom,) some nations were conquered and colonised, (the Northern Kingdom of Israel is an example) hence the colonised nation is bound to take the culture of the colonisers. So culture might change slightly to take the culture of the colonisers.

THE GENTILES WANTED TO BE CHRISTIANS MORE THAN THE JEWS BECAUSE THEY NEVER BOASTED AS A CHOSEN PEOPLE:

The term gentile originally means those people who are none Jews, the reason why most of them are Christians is that they have no reservations. It is becoming more and more difficult for the Jews to convert to Christianity because they say that they are the chosen people, so they are not easily convinced that Christianity is as godly as they think they are. To start with, the Jews tried to resist the gentiles coming to Christianity, when they failed to stop that, they started themselves to resent being Christians, hence the gentiles outnumbered them that they started saying it is a gentile movement. Anybody who fears God and does what he wants is the one that will be accepted in the kingdom of God. The Lord does not have a special nation that is the reason why gentiles are following Him. For most of gentiles to become Christians was of God's own making, because as we learn from what happened, it is clear in some cases. We have examples of gentiles receiving the Holy Spirit without first going through the Jewish culture. This did not go well with the Jews who thought they were the chosen nation

JESUS DISCUSSES WITH THE PHARISEES AND SADDUCEES ABOUT THEIR CULTURE:

In(Matthew 23) (KJV), Jesus said to the Pharisees, by trying to perfect Moses' laws, they ended up being carried away. That is the reason why when they were discussing issue with Jesus, they were always conflicting with Him because they expected Him to agree with them. What Christ went through is what today's Christian is going through, they arm twist the Christians so that they bow to their gods. This time, it is done in such a way that it may not be noticed, because the devil is becoming more and more tactful.

Jesus said to them, the Law of Moses was given by God yes, (which served as their culture) but the Pharisees added their own or extended these laws to suit themselves. They wanted others to obey them, when they themselves did not. That is the reason why Jesus said culture had to be kept in check by Christianity: Some drawbacks that culture might encounter are that culture is transmitted verbally from one generation to the other. In the transition, one might add or subtract to suit them. So that is the way it may lose some of its value along the way. The reason why culture has to be kept in check is that it might get out of hand. He gave as an example the Law of Moses, some very religious Pharisees were moving about wearing the law on their forehead or as an arm band tied around their arms, to show people that they keep these laws. They were showing off that they keep their culture more than others.

Jesus warned them against washing cups outside, when inside they were very dirty. When washing a cup outside only, you would like it to appear to people like it is very clean, giving a negative impression of it. Jesus wants us to examine our hearts because those are the inside of our cups, for the

Lord examines our hearts. This teaches us how we should be, if we want to be acceptable to God. Before we make any judgement on someone else, we have to examine our hearts, secure, how our own assumed position is, according to Pharisees, sincerity does not matter, you may be extremely sincere, and yet sincerely wrong. What is called a person is inside of us, that is where the Lord examines us, so we should always keep in check whether our inside is pleasing to the Lord.

CHRISTIANITY-JEWISH RECONCILIATION:

(*myjewishlearnig.com*) accessed 27 April 2020) during the time of Christian persecution, (by the Jews) the relationship between Judaism and Christianity were badly strained in such a way that it is needs healing. Life will not be bearable to continue like this for ever. That is the reason why there is required some reconciliation. It will serve no purpose at all to continue like this because from the look of things, what happened that some had a revelation and accepted the Messiahship of Christ while some did not, will not change yet good relationship is required, that is the reason why both sides have to compromise in order to have good relationship in future and forget the past. There are some radicals today, who would say, but Christians were badly treated, they were killed for the sake of Christianity. If we are emulating Jesus, He was also killed when He was not at fault, but for our own sake. He said whoever wants to follow me must take up his cross and follow me. Those are the words we are obeying and following His foot-steps. It will serve no purpose if we do like Peter who wanted a revenge to those who were arresting Christ when he cut the ear of one of those who were arresting Him, but Jesus Himself said to Peter it is never done like that, and He put the ear back and healed His enemy. Christian-Jewish reconciliation refers to the efforts that are being made to improve understanding and acceptance by Christians of Jewish people and Judaism and to eliminate Christian antisemitism and anti-Judaism. There has been significant progress in reconciliation in recent years, particularly from so many Christian beliefs and also by other Christian groups. During the second Temple period there was a split between the Jews themselves because some Jews did not take the teachings of Jesus, They refused to accept Him and His teachings that they even agreed that He must be crucified, which they did and thought that they had silenced Him. To their surprise He rose from the dead and ascended to heaven. There were some Jews who believed in Him, but they were also hated like they had hated Jesus. The hatred became very big when those who believed in the Messiah had accepted the gentiles into Christianity, because the thought they were the chosen people. Now that Christianity has grown to be the world religion, they the Jews are the ones asking for reconciliation because they can see that they are being taken by events. Where the reconciliation is being concentrated on is the fact that the Jews had resisted Christianity in such a way that they persecuted Christians until they were scatted all-over the world but kept on spreading the Christian movement until it became the world religion. Christians are looking back and seeing the covenant that God made with Abraham, and also that God does not change His covenant. He said to Abraham that every nation that will bless you will also be blessed. Two thousand years of resentment Christians are saying there must be some reconciliation. Although there is a new covenant, but Jesus said He did not come to do away with the old but to work with it in such a way that they will all work together, the old and the new.

THERE IS NEED TO IMPROVE RELATIONS BETWEEN CHRISTIANITY AND JUDAISM:

Although Christianity originated from Judaism, this means some Jews quickly accepted the Messiahship of Jesus but some did not, it now appears there is tension between those who accepted and those who did not accept. As Christianity spread at a faster rate in those early days, Christians should always keep on praying to be filled with the Holy Spirit so that they can be able to do their duties without fear as the Lord promised that He would be with all those who will go about spreading the word. As civilisation improves there is an improvement between Judaism and Christianity the reason being that people want to solve their differences peacefully other than having tensions between them. On the other hand, inter marriage has also been a contributing factor; this is because the times have changed, because early in their history the Jews never wanted to inter marry.

THERE HAS TO BE RE-EVALUATION OF CHRISTIAN ATTITUDE TOWARDS JEWS IN ORDER TO NORMALISE THE CURRENT RELATIONSHIP:

ANTI-SEMITISM AND ANTI-JUDAISM FROM CHRISTIANS IS BEING DISCOURAGED BUT IS STILL PERSISTING:

If Christianity is to win the souls of those who are not yet Christians, then Christianity has to employ new methods or a new approach. It appears those who should be exemplary to show what are themselves being diluted other than applying methods that those who are outside would like follow the movement. This means that Christians in their life application should make people want to be Christians. If in some countries Christianity might appear like there is growth, it has to be looked at closely, may be those churches are being filled with people who come with different motives. If the church is filled with people who realise that God is Spirit and those who worship Him must worship Him in Spirit and in truth, then the people shall know that there is something worth going to church for. Christians have a task to separate religion, ritual and Christianity so that when they stand clear of each other, people will know what to choose. Where the trap lies is that we are not able to separate socioeconomic and politics from religion and move on with them alongside each other without interfering with each other.

JESUS DISCUSSES JEWISH LAW WITH THE PHARISEES:

The Pharisees regarded these laws as their culture, so they were in disagreement with Jesus thinking that he was trying to move them away from their culture. Jesus wanted them to be pure in their hearts instead of worrying about the law. Jesus was saying that he was not against their laws, but that they must be pure in their hearts. This teaches us that it is not enough to show to people that you are a Christian without being pure in our hearts, at the anointing of David; God said he looks at the heart. Sometimes instead of being against Jesus they turned to disagree among themselves, like what was happening between the Pharisees and the Sadducees, they disagreed on the observance of the Sabbath. The

Pharisees received the support of the people as compared to the Sadducees who regarded themselves as a top class.

THE CHRISTIAN VIEW OF THE TRANSITION FROM JUDAISM TO CHRISTIANITY:

(John 1:1-4) (KJV), changing from Judaism to Christianity is that some understood the Messiahship of Jesus, but some did not. In the earliest Gospel texts, which pictured Jesus as debating issues of Jewish law with the Pharisees no hostility is observed? The crucifixion is said to have been carried out by the Romans with support of some (apparently Hellenized) priests as we traced the history of the New Testament traditions, they move from disputes with Pharisees and scribes and chief priests (all members of various second temple-era Jewish sects) to Polemics against the Jews and Judaism, from the notion of Jews as enemies of Jesus to the demonization of Jewish people as a whole.

WE TRANSITION FROM JUDAISM TO CHRISTIANITY, BY ACCEPTING THE NEW COVENANT:

The Jews did not understand the Messiahship of Jesus Christ. They nursed a grudge with Jesus until they plotted to kill Him, they falsely accused He until they brought Him for trial, was sentenced to death which He was killed by crucifixion, and they said they had silenced Him, to their surprise He rose from the dead and ascended to heaven, but they started persecuting His followers that they were scattered, started churches wherever they went that gave Christianity a chance to grow. The biggest difference that made them to separate quickly was when the Christians had started to bring it the gentiles in to the church, then those who followed Christ were barred from using the synagogues anymore. They started meeting in the open until they started building their own churches as Christians. Christianity started by spreading through the Roman Empire until some governments started recognising Christianity as a religion to become the official religion of the Roman Empire. After Christ had left, Christianity began as a Jewish sect, the more the Christians were persecuted, the more it spread. The Jews believe in the participation as individuals in prayer and believing that there they reject the concept of Christianity that of **taking them as a trinity.**

THE PHARISEES OR JEWS DID NOT UNDERSTAND THE MESSIAHSHIP OF JESUS:

There are some pointers to the coming of the Messiah such as in Genesis 49:10 where it is said that the Messiah would come from the tribe of Judah. In (2 Samuel 7:12-16) (KJV) David is assured that from his descendant there will raise a king who will rule for ever. (1 Chronicles 22:9-10) (KJV); (John 4:25-26) (KJV) Sometimes in our lives when something come to us or when something happens we tend to politicise it such as the time of the coming of the Messiah, the were under colonial rule from the Romans, so the quickly jumped into the conclusion that He was going to liberate them from the rule of the Romans. What added to the confusion was that there were some who claimed that they were messiahs such as Rabbi Akiva who declared Shimon bar Kokhba as messiah in 135.

THE JEWISH VIEW OF CHRISTIANITY:

In its very earliest days, the Jewish teachers saw Christianity as a heresy: its adherence was Jews who believed in the divinity of Christ (and considered Christianity a Jewish sect). However, when Christianity spread and became a world religion, it became a rival with numerous converts from gentile world; it became the rival religion to Judaism. Christians were seen as gentiles not because they are Christians but because, in the main, they were gentiles (not Jews).

Christianity did not come so easily or quickly, to change from Judaism to Christianity was not that simple, before that, when Jesus was debating with them, they thought that Jesus was trying to make them abandon their culture. Yet Jesus was quite clear on that when he said to them that he did not come to do away with the law, but to fulfil it. This they did not quite get at first because this kind of saying requires divine revelation to understand what Jesus meant. It appears this is currently affecting us this present day, where we fall into the same trap as the Pharisees. The Jews thought that the Gentiles were the unchosen, but the gentiles received the Holy Spirit without first going through the Jewish culture. Those Jews, who were early Christians, found themselves caught in between, wanting to adopt the Christian faith, and wanting to adhere to their Jewish culture. This has set a pace for our life application, as it appears that today's Christianity is falling into that temptation which befell those early Jews. This is the reason why this book is trying to help in decision making. The term "Jewish-Christian" appears in historical texts contrasting Christians of Jewish origin. Some of the reasons why they would not believe in him are that they lost focus on the Messiahship. By thinking that theirs was the only culture that should be followed, made them to be unpopular among the gentiles.

THE EARLY JEWS THOUGHT THAT THEY COULD CONTROL CHRISTIANITY:

In its earliest days, Jewish teachers saw Christianity as a Jewish heresy. They very much resented to what Christianity was trying to bring; the dualism of God: to say God the Father and God the Son. They based their argument on (Isaiah 44:6) (KJV) which says I am the first, and I am the last, and besides Me there is no God for I have no son, no brother besides Me there is no other. They expanded on (Isiah 44:6) (KJV) and give the revelation of it. It was not until the middle ages that the status of Christianity "and of Islam" as a rival religion was considered from the Jewish point of view.

As it started to dominate, Jewish Teachers take Christianity as a heresy:

Christianity was taken as heresy by the Jewish teachers because their teaching was from God they never adapted to change, although they had seen what Christ had done, they never could give it a thought, they had never recognised Him as the Messiah. Christianity is guided by the Holy Spirit as promised by Jesus before His ascension and as what happened at Pentecost. Christianity has become a world religion, and it still spreading. Christianity was said to be heresy because it became a teaching contrary to originally held belief.

CHAPTER 14

The Christian religion became a rival to Judaism because the Jews were always at variance with Jesus:

The gentiles believe in Christianity more than Jews because they have no other religion to boast about:

JEWISH CHRISTIAN RELATIONSHIP TODAY:

Christianity is rooted in Second Temple Judaism,(that is, when the Jerusalem Temple was rebuilt after the return from exile) but the two religions diverged in the first century of the Christian era. Christianity emphasises on the correct belief focusing on the new covenant as mediated through Jesus Christ, as recorded in the New Testament. Judaism places emphasis on right conduct focusing on the Mosaic Covenant, as recorded in the Torah and Talmud. Christians believe in individual salvation from sin through repentance and receiving Jesus Christ as their God and Saviour through faith in Jesus Christ. Jews believe in individual and collective participation in an internal dialogue with God through tradition, rituals, prayers and ethical actions. Christianity generally believes in a Triune God, one Person of whom became human. Judaism emphasises on oneness of God and rejects the Christian concept of God in human form.

JESUS FACES OPPOSITION FROM RELIGIOUS LEADERS:

Religious leaders in the gospels always accused Jesus of wanting to do away with their culture. (John 15:20) (KJV). A servant is not greater than his master is: if they persecuted me, they will persecute you also. The fact is that these Pharisees were really not clean in their hearts, while Jesus was divine. Although He had two natures, human nature and divine nature, they failed to defile His human nature. As these were two different things that they were corrupt in their hearts and Jesus was divine and perfect, they hated Him more. As they never wanted to repent, Jesus showed no grace for them. He always pointed out to them that they were hypocritical, which strained their relationship even worse; they never liked Him for exposing their inner feelings. Their hatred to Him was not founded, but that could not make Him lose His goodness. Their characters to the people were exposed, which made them hate Him more. It appears it is still following that which happened that their deeds were exposed and they hated Jesus. When Christianity exposes dirty deeds we start crying foul, and start saying Christianity has killed our culture. That has been inherited by this generation; they do not want Christianity to point out what they may be doing wrong. Yet before the exposure, they commanded some respect and were prestigious. As a result, they nursed a grudge against Jesus, which kept on growing as time passed, this grudge kept on growing until it reached a stage where they agreed He must be crucified.

CHAPTER 15

THERE ARE SOME SIMILARITIES IN DIFFERENT CULTURES:

The faiths of the people may be different depending on what culture they are in. Different cultures have different faiths. Do we celebrate cultural similarities, or they are over taken by cultural differences? If we could focus on cultural similarities and build on that; we would be taking those differences and find common ground on the similarities that exist. That is trying to find a common ground and build something positive. Because of the changing times, people of different cultures are finding themselves working together, yet before they worked together they had different values. Now that they have a common ground they have to forego their differences. When working with someone who values things differently, try to find a common ground.

THE TRANSITION FROM JUDAISM TO CHRISTIANITY IS COMPLEX:

With the fact that God made a covenant with Abraham, that he would be father of many nations, it did not click to them that God was for all. The transition is complex in that changing from Judaism to Christianity was a revolution which cannot take place in a day. When it was preached that Christ was crucified and buried, and rose from the dead, some believed but some did not. So it required to be spiritually filled in order to be able to convince people that this is the truth. That is why it was a process not an event. The other reason why many Jews could not follow Christianity was that more gentiles became Christians more than Jews, and also that they thought it was killing their culture by not observing some of the laws of Moses; (circumcision was an example).

For quite some time there was a difference between Judaism and Christianity, the Christians wanted to attract more Jews into Christianity. This was a simple reason that Jesus was a Jew, and was of Jewish culture, chose all his disciples from the Jewish community. So people went all along with that culture, but went on to add something like, Jesus Christ was the messiah, but some doubted and they kept on thinking that the Messiah has still to come, up to this present day. It required a lot of teaching to convince those who were in Judaism that Christianity was a movement based on the faith that there was the resurrection of Christ, and there is going to be the resurrection of the dead that die in Christ. That is the reason why some are still holding on to the belief that the Messiah is still to come. Most of them thought of him as a political leader. During Jesus' time, the Jews were under Roman rule, yet Jesus was condemned to death and crucified under Roman rule. According to them, where was his power?

The first Jewish-Roman war was in 66AD. In 70 AD there was the destruction of the temple. This brought mixed feelings: some thought it was a punishment for not following Christ but, some thought they were not following properly the teaching of the Torah. The development of the New Testament helped the belief in Christianity.

Christianity differed from Judaism in that Judaism was for the Jews only, taking themselves as the chosen people. Whereas, Christianity is the religion of every one, rich or poor, young and old, male or female, Gentile or Jew. According to Jesus everyone was now free to go to the Lord through him alone.

COMPARE CHRISTIANITY TO ISLAM:

Christianity: God is one in Three Persons; Father, Son and Holy Spirit.

Islam: Allah is one; he has no son. The Holy Spirit does not exist.

Christianity: All Biblical Scripture is inspired by God and useful to teach us what is true, to abide by its unchanging words brings peace of mind and up lifting of the spirit.

Islam: Jews and Christians corrupted the Bible by removing verses that foretold Muhammad's coming and added verses to establish Jesus' divinity.

Christianity: The Bible was canonized in AD325 some 300 years before Islam was founded. No Muslim existed or could have existed at that time.

Islam: All Biblical prophets were Muslims, including Abraham, Noah, Moses and Jesus. Adam was a Muslim.

Christianity: God is Personal.

Islam: Allah is unknowable.

Christianity: God loves all people, including Muslims.

Islam: Allah hates apostates and blasphemers. Allah and God are one and the same.

JUMPTO: HOME BELIEFS HISTORY GROWTH FAQs SELF-TESTS GET BOOK CONTACT.

Christianity: God says there will be no liars in heaven: (Revelations 21:8) (KJV).

Islam: Allah says, if a Muslim feels threatened, it may be necessary to lie, break treaties or deny their faith. (Qur'an 8:8: 16:106).

Christianity: God commands all people to love Him and love one another, even their enemies.

<u>Islam:</u> Allah commands Muslims to fight them on until there is no more tumult or oppression (Qur'an 8:39).

<u>Christianity:</u> Jesus said, stop judging others and you will not be judge, (Matthew 7:1) (KJV).

<u>Islam:</u> Allah give Muslims the ability and authority to judge between men, (Qur'an 4:105; 5:49).w

CHAPTER 16

CHRISTIANS SHOULD BE INVOLVED IN CULTURE IN SUCH A WAY THAT THEY WILL NOT BE CORRUPTED:

CHRISTIANS SHOULD INVOLVE THEMSELVES IN CULTURE IN SUCH A WAY THAT THEY WILL BE ABLE TO ACHIEVE THEIR GOAL:

The best way Christians would achieve their goal is ensure that the people receive as much of civilisation education as they could, because the more the people are civilise, the more they are able to differentiate good from bad, and the difference between primitively and civilised life. So people must be educated in such a way that they are able to choose for themselves what is good for them and what is not.

THE EARLY CHRISTIANS WERE ABLE TO PRESERVE CHRISTIANITY FROM CULTURE THROUGH THE HELP OF THE HOLY SIRIT:

The early church had a great task in ensuring that people received some form of education. Most of the very early schools were under missionary care, although of late most governments have taken over the responsibility of educating young people. A credit must be given to Christianity for taking the lead. Most of the social services like schools and hospitals were under the care of the early church. By enlightening the people through education, people were able to make choices as to what aspects of culture to go along with and what aspects to leave out. To educate people is to empower them with the knowledge which makes them to be able to make a choice for themselves. Equip people with education and they are able to tell and to take what is good for them. This does not stop some forces of darkness from trying to destabilise the light which was said in (John chapter 1:4-5) (KJV) this means, without His light we are stumbling in darkness. The only way to get out of this darkness is to allow His light to shine in us, and we will be following in His footsteps. His footsteps are that He underwent persecution, which we are also going through, yet He suffered this until the end at the cross when all hopes of all those who had no revelation were lost. Then suddenly, the resurrection brought all light to mankind, and the darkness was unable to conceal the light anymore. The writer is pleading with the reader to strive to have this light shown in them to ensure that any kind of darkness will not come near them in the name of Jesus Christ our Lord and saviour. So it is not a matter of culture being killed, but about people being educated and being able to make the right choices.

Even those who are not Christians accepted to go along with festivals like Christmas and Easter. The establishment of schools did not end with primary or secondary education only, but went to as far as universities; which have taken education to a higher notch. The cultural diversities although they make no mention of any Christianity, they may be taking their example from Jesus' parable of the Good Samaritan. Those who ask for equality are saying, human beings are equal in the eyes of God, so the Good Samaritan has taken the lead in saying that all human beings are equal as shown by his action. Even the human rights activists get their notion from that parable. The courts make their oaths from the Bible, (although here and there they may deviate from it). Ethics although no mention of it, may also be guided by the Bible.

CHAPTER 17

THE ROMAN GOVERNMENT DID NOT UNDERSTAND JESUS' KINGSHIP AND HIS MESSIAHSHIP AND COULD NOT KNOW WHICH LEGAL STATUS TO GIVE HIM:

Jesus was a Jew and of a Jewish culture, so it was difficult for the Romans to understand His kingship and His Messiahship. To Jesus it was a double edged sword. Even on Jesus' trial, Pilate did not know who He was, that is why pilate was asking: "Are you the king of the Jews?" On the one hand the Jews hated His miraculous way of doing things and the Romans on the other hand did not understand Him, (because they were not a chosen people). They could only hear the Jews calling Him king of the Jews. To start with, He was not known to the Romans because He only concentrated among the Jewish community. There were mixed feelings also even among the Jews themselves, for some when they heard that He was king of the Jews they took Him as a political leader, expecting Him to liberate them from Roman colonial rule, of which He did not meet their expectations. When He did not meet their expectations, He was condemned and sentenced to death by the rule of the Romans, crucified and really died. Then all their hopes of His followers were dashed. The growth of Christianity only came after the resurrection when He promised the coming of the Holy Spirit, which empowered all the apostles handing the power down to us. That is when Christianity began to spread and grow which was not to the expectation of anyone. Paul had an assignment to go to the gentiles, which he did and made the gospel to spread to all the Roman empire, since they were taken unawares, they wanted to stop its spread, but it was too late, this kind of thinking can still be seen to this present day as there are some who still want Christianity off the face of the earth, something that may not happen. The Holy Spirit is empowering Christian more than ever before to have it spread all over the globe. Right now there are some countries which are very resistive to the spread of Christianity, but if the Lord so wishes His people to know His word, they could be swimming against the tide. The main purpose of Paul's letters is to tell every believer and non-believers that there will be a resurrection after death. Which Christ Himself set as an example, because He Himself was crucified, died and was buried, but rose from the dead and is now alive. It is evidence that when it is preached that there will be the resurrection of the dead there is proof.

THE ROMAN CULTURE WAS DIFFERENT FROM THE JEWISH CULTURE, THAT IS THE REASON WHY THERE WAS ALWAYS SOME DISAGREEMENT:

The Jews very much liked their culture to dominate because they thought they were the chosen people. For them to be ruled by the Romans and sometimes being made to follow the Roman culture because they were under the Roman colonial rule was difficult to swallow for the Jews. You imagine being made to take foreign culture, you are identified by your culture, and you are proud of it .Constantine gave Christianity a boost when he recognised Christianity as a religion. Why would the Jews ever think of revolting against the Roman rule yet when caught trying to revolt, the punishment was very heavy.

They could be forced to take some of the aspects of foreign culture that the Jews could be compelled by the Romans because they were the rulers. For that to be done to Jews, they thought that their culture was being trodden under foot of man. There is enough evidence to show that they could adopt some foreign culture because they were exiled to Babylon Asia Minor some to Rome because the Jews could be scattered in the diaspora, because the situation forced them to.

THE JOHANNINE COMMUNITY EVADED PERSECUTION IN ORDER TO PRESERVE CHRISTIANITY:

The transition from Judaism to Christianity did not come so easily. Originally these people shared the same belief and the same culture. But with the fact that some had a revelation and recognised that Jesus was the Messiah, they began to differ in culture and religious thinking better than their colleagues who had no revelation. It can be imagined what they went through, different opinions but still using the same synagogue. Those Jews, who were the first to be Christians, saw a bright future in Christianity. So as they continued to differ in their beliefs, it would come to a stage where they would no longer use the same synagogue, with varying beliefs, so Christians were expelled from the synagogue. What these Christians were doing showed much success, where their colleagues were not succeeding this did not go very well with their colleagues; at the destruction of the Jerusalem temple which was their centre of worship, but their Christian colleagues referred to John 4:21 which refers to God who is not a physical being who can only be found in the Jerusalem Temple, yet God is Spirit, whoever wants to truly worship Him must worship Him in Spirit and in truth. In AD70, the Romans added the tension, the Jews knew that God could only be worshiped in one place, while Christians know that God is Spirit and can be worshiped anywhere, in truth and in Spirit. The inclusion of the gentiles made the tension even worse because they believed that they were the chosen people of God, while the Christian Jews knew that in the eyes of God there was no gentile or Jew, one love of all. That made the Jewish Christians to drift apart from the mainstream Judaism, hence Christianity spread while Judaism was shrinking. (John 19:22; 12:42) (KJV), this tension between the Jews did not start there, but had started while Jesus was still on His mission on earth they were always arguing with Him that their tension led to the crucifixion of Jesus, and (Acts 19:8) (KJV), that tension went on because the Jews never accepted that there was anything that would be accepted by God other than the law of Moses, yet these apostles knew that man could be saved by grace alone and not by following the law of Moses. As a result of this tension, they were expelled from the synagogues. Their expulsion had a positive effect, since they could now concentrate on Christianity other than mixing with

Judaism. We have to bear in mind that this was the work of the Holy Spirit. To appear like things are going the wrong way, yet it is for the growth of Christianity, watch our life application.

The Johannine Community could no longer be associates of the Jews, it was because of their knowledge of the gospel, and they became very controversial. The other factor of their expulsion was they were becoming different from their colleagues because they were communicating with the outside world such as gentiles which offended the Jews even more. Christianity is for the people, so they are trying to reach out to people. It was not easy for the Johannine Community; those who were expelled were some who were half hearted. Even today we should avoid being half-hearted in our Christian faith. Sometimes for them not to be persecuted, they employed the tactic of assimilation in order to avoid being separatists, who they could be identified easily, but in their hearts knowing fully well that Jesus was the Messiah, Nicodimus is an example.

THE GOSPEL OF JOHN WAS WRITTEN IN ORDER TO SHOW THAT JESUS OF NAZARETH WAS THE MESSIAH:

(Cliffsnotes.com) The purpose of the Gospel of John being written was, s stated by John himself, was to show that Jesus of Nazareth was Christ, the Son of God, and that believers in Him might have eternal life. Although the four synoptic Gospels were similar in their approach of the teachings and the works of Jesus Christ, John found that there were some materials that were left out by the other Gospels, but which appears in his Gospel alone, like the wedding at Cana of Galilee, the Samaritan woman at the well and also: and that the second coming of Jesus was real, and that there was eternal life. He brought his message in such a way that one who would take that word and understand it, and live accordingly, would receive eternal life. His gospel was to bring the message that the one who believes in Him will also receive power and will also be living according to His to live according to His word brings transformation in our lives, which when we are transformed and be like Him who is like His Father, which means we will have joined the trinity. John was an eye witness of

Jesus' mission here on earth that led him to write in order for us to have first-hand information, and to show that Jesus Christ of Nazareth was the true Messiah. To let the people know that the coming of the kingdom of Jesus is imminent, and also to let people know that He was there in the beginning as word and that the word became flesh. There is a strong connection between divine and human, which relationship the writer says should be maintained, the writer wants the people to be really transformed. He pleads with all human beings to ask for the indwelling of the Holy Spirit for without it life is meaningless, because if it indwells in us we become transformed creatures. The writer urges us to have a linkage which Jesus said Him and His Father are one, so He wants us to be connected to him so that as a result we will be also connected to the Father. He wants all Christians to note that the persecution that Jesus faced was also faced by the early apostles, which have been handed down to us, so we must be strengthened spiritually when we suffer these things as Christians.

THE BOOK OF REVELATIONS WAS WRITTEN AS A WARNING FOR THE SECOND COMING OF CHRIST:

The Book of Revelations was written by John the disciple when he was on the Island of Patmos. It was written as a warning for the second coming of Christ which we seem to heed very lightly. John was commanded to write these things because they are true Jesus told him (Revelations 1:10-11) (KJV) "I am Alpha and Omega the first and the last", this book was written to warn us that there is definitely a second coming, which we seem to be ignoring because we do not have a divine revelation which this book is pleading with the reader to ask for that revelation in order to see what is in the future, in order to stay alert and stay connected. Let us put our faith and hope in it for it was made in order to save our souls. The problem we are facing is that we seem to think that on the judgement day we will be very intelligent to answer questions satisfactorily, yet on judgement day all our deeds will be displayed, you look at them and judge yourself, because there will be no time for repentance, for time for repentance is now while grace and mercy are still available. There will be no time for that, only that there will be gnashing of teeth. This book should prepare and strengthen our Christian beliefs. Forces of darkness will always come and they want to sway us from the truth. God very much wants to reveal Himself to us if we seek Him whole heartedly. Like today's people, some people of those days had become lukewarm that they very much compromised Christianity. If you read and understand this book for it might lead you into eternal life. This book is preparing us for the time that time of tribulation.

ALL CHRISTIAN REVELATION IS PRESERVED IN THE BIBLE:

Sometimes scriptures are not as straight as they are but sometimes we have the truth. In the beginning of the Bible, God reveals Himself as an intelligent Creator of intelligent creatures (mankind). God Himself started communicating with a man. We have to expect God to still do the same as He did before God was communicating; He is still communicating with us today. God is revealed in the Bible, so the source of knowing God is the Bible. Although the Bible does not mention the Trinity, it does reveal the relationship that exists among them. (Ephesians 3:14-15) (KJV) as we believe in God we become one family God promises love and power to His family, so we are asking everyone not to cut themselves from the true [and happy family. Let pray without seizing so that we keep connected to the true vine. As Jesus says I am the true vine everyone who is in me will bear fruit, those who are off have cut themselves off and no one else if we are in Jesus and Jesus is in the Trinity that means we will also be in the Trinity that means we one family Of God .The canonisation of the Bible helped to preserve Christianity. Through the deed of God Himself, the Bible has been preserved such that it has been able to survive history that it has been there for over 4000 years. As a result of canonisation, the Bible has become a Holy Scripture. There is divine inspiration in the Bible God Himself commanded these scriptures to be done that is why they stay sacred at all time.

THE HELLENISTIC CULTURE RULED THE KNOWN WORLD THAT TIME:

Culture could be said to be different from Christianity in that whichever nation was conquering that period, their culture would dominate .Like during the period of 323BC THE Greeks were a dominant nation, so the Hellenistic culture was also dominating. This was dominant until when the Roman rule took over in 146 BC everything was required to identify with the Greek world and apply the Greek ideologies. During those periods of wars, any nation that would have conquered and was ruling, could make other nations under it to take their culture. That is the reason why when the Greeks nearly ruled the whole world that time, the Hellenistic culture was dominant during that period. So the Greek language was dominant as well as the Hellenistic culture.

THE INTER -TESTAMENTAL PERIOD WAS DOMINATED BY THE HELLENISTIC CULTURE:

(The Transformed Soul) (By Dr.D.W. Ekstrand)There was a time known as the inter-testament period when God did not directly communicate with people as He used to do during the times like the time of Moses when He could sometimes speak directly to individuals or to groups, this is the time of the close of the Old Testament and the beginning of the New Testament. (That is about 425 BC) That is the time when the chosen people were undergoing from one colonial rule to the other, like from Persian rule to the Babylonian captivity to the Roman Empire. They intermixed with the Hellenists who greatly influenced their culture. Sometime we fail to understand the way God works, it could be because sometimes we may want to claim to know Him when it is better for us to humble ourselves before Him, because some of these happenings of this period, he had said it when He prefigured the coming of the Saviour. Sometimes Jesus kept on reminding His disciples that these things were said before up to this date we seem to be surprised with the things that were said before. It would be advisable for us to seek His revelation and guidance in order to recognise His great ness. (Revelations 1:1-20) says it all how and why it was written and that it is for the saving of our souls.

WHAT IS AGREED AS THE NORM OF THE CULTURE BECOMES THE MORALITY OF CULTURE:

The values of culture as agreed to by society, in turn makes the morality of culture, as long as society agrees that this is the norm of their culture. The rules that govern the behaviours of society in order to guide it along become the norms of the society. There are some rules that are found to be good to be followed in order to have a well dignified society, once they are found to build a nation; they then become the norms of that society. Values are general guide lines, while norms are specific guide lines. There are certain things that are not enforced by anyone but just happen automatically, for example, some set aside colours for different genders, and also such as, women are more caring than men without anyone telling them to behave that way. Such things become the norms of the society, without anyone, each member of society is expected to conform to those rules having been formulated by them. Without anyone having to enforce them, as long as everyone agrees that this is the best way to go about them, they will become norms. Once society agrees that this is normal, it then becomes the norm of that society, without needing to make it law. There are rules that govern and guide a society, if they are followed, in turn they will make that society. What is in a person that makes them to be able to distinguishing between good and bad right and wrong behaviour? We always need guidance in our lives in order to know which path to follow, our actions are either right or wrong actions, and we always ask to be guided to take the right action. The shared concepts and beliefs will guide and regulate culture or community so they become a morality.

When people live in a group they create a code, it is called as morality, it is something formulated that a group of people want to follow within their community. When these people migrate to different places and they want to follow that it is called a culture. Some of the codes can be acceptable, some of them will be stupid blind faith and maybe valid in that group only where it originated and only during that time. In the river of life some are stuck in stagnant pools. Our culture greatly contributes to our or to the development of our beliefs and values. For this reason both cultural and psychologists and social anthropologists believe that culture affects one's personality. In addition gender differences also influence the personality traits a person possesses.

HUMAN NATURE SOMETIMES MISLEAD CULTURE:

It appears like they are failing to separate the two with clear cut explanation, we cannot speak of one and exclude the other, and they seem to be interwoven. However the research goes on in order to have a clear-cut definition. Human nature could be called characteristics such as a way of thinking or way of behaving feelings and acting, some of these things happen naturally, without thinking or waiting to be told. There is a thin separation between human nature and human biology, these two are joined together to make human behaviour. We must first of all be able to define and distinguish the difference between human nature and human culture. "human nature" Human nature is a general psychological characteristics, feelings, and behavioural traits of humankind, regarded as shared by all humans, including ways of thinking, feeling, and acting, which humans have naturally. "Human culture"

CULTURE SHOULD HAVE A GOOD RELATIONSHIP
WITH CHRISTIANITY, CHRIST AND GOD:

Sometimes we just follow culture as a norm; our day to day living is the norm of culture, so some of the things we do in culture will just happen automatically, without giving it a push or a thought. The only time that may make us deviate from the norm is the fact that most of the cultural things are verbal; there are some elements who would like to do things their own way, which might make some of the aspects of culture to be corrupted, therefore needing Christianity to cleanse them. We just follow it without asking questions. There are different sets of values in different cultures, this follows generation after generation. The values of culture are the core principles, and where the nation bases their faith on, their customs rituals traditions depending on what that group believes in. As an example, to the Hindu culture, no matter how hungry they might be a cow is sacred to them, which means they are able to sacrifice their lives than eating a cow Sometimes our values may conflict with God's will, since God is Spirit, so we must ensure that what we do culturally conforms to the will of God because God is supreme. We all know God is the supreme, as culture evolves from generation to generation, as culture evolves from one generation to the other, it might lose some of its values or might have some slight changes since the changes are a free will, sometimes these changes might be gradual they may not be as rapid as could be visible or to be quick and taking a long time, sometimes it is transmitted from one generation to the next generation by means of teaching the siblings, the language customs or behaviour, but God never changes. People are not to follow the pattern of this world but to follow God's will. We have so many different cultures of this world, but we only have one God's will. We have a very good example, (Romans 12:2) (KJV) says it all, where it says God has plans for us all when He takes what is bad from us. Christians are not to be conformed to this world but to conform to the will of God.

THE BIBLE SHOULD REVEAL THE TRUTH THAT IS THERE ABOUT CULTURE OR CHRISTIANITY:

Sometimes we want to read the Bible with preconceived ideas, yet the Bible should guide us so that we can understand it, when reading scriptures ask the Lord for revelation, because He is the one who inspired its compilation. It is not advisable to try to put the Bible in our own way, instead of following it as it is. Let us not try to put God's creation. (Mark 7:13) (KJV) Thus you nullify the word of God by your tradition which you handed down we should always ask God to renew us from within us. Christians are urged not to be defiled by this world because this world is a corrupt world. Sometimes we have a desire to follow worldly things because they appear attractive and so tempting that we have to ask for guidance, because of that we may be led into sinning. Do not allow the world to lead you into its own ways, but keep attached to your Father who is in heaven. Do not be conformed to this world, but be transformed by the renewal of your mind, that by testing you may discern what the will of God is, what is good and acceptable and perfect. Since Jesus said you are the salt of the world, it means we cannot be separated from them but that as a Christian, when mixing with them we must not be diluted or carried away but to try to make them to be conformed to Christ. God reveals Himself through the scriptures, so to know Him better we must always be consulting the scriptures. Christianity influences culture (ohn 8:32) (KJV) it is always advisable to be always truthful for the truth will never change. Jesus wants us to be truthful as He was because He came here to set an example to us to follow. The whole aim is to transform culture by applying Christian principles, in the end the relationship that is built is a sound relationship. Christianity is based on the birth, teachings, death and resurrection of Christ, which we would call, is our guide lines to guide us into eternal life, which the main aim of Christianity, (John 18:38) (KJV).

MORAL ABSOLUTE SHOULD BE BASED ON ABSOLUTE TRUTH:

A moral truth is a description of action which has some implications, in our lives and teaches people how to live their lives and what makes good or bad action. The principles that guide us in our lives in order to make us full human beings, in other words, it is a true living. Truth and morality could go hand in hand because they both try to make a person's life a perfect life lived to its fullest extent. A person must always live life honestly, which in the end will keep the morality which in the end, is living life to its fullness which is only found in true living. Absolute truth is the inflexible reality, fixed, invariable, unalterable facts. There are some who would like to dig into. Sometimes we find such truths in Christianity, but the atheists would like to argue on that, saying there is no such thing as absolute truth.

Always the truth is the fact of the matter which is never disputed; the truth will always be the truth no matter what circumstances it goes through. It appears today's society does not care about telling the truth, yet it is better to love things that agree with reality, such as the truth. Always supressing the truth gives a false conclusion.

THERE IS A GOOD RELATIONSHIP BETWEEN MORALITY AND CULTURE:

Morals differ as cultures differ from one culture to the other but the bottom line is, every culture has their own morality. Each culture looks at its own people, it has got something they say, if such a culture or if such kind of behaviour is followed, we will be a well behaved culture, when viewed by the other cultures. There is no universal in cultural morality, as they all differ in their approach, and their way of behaviour. Cultural dynamics are hugely influential in establishing and propagating mores and generating normative moral frameworks. This is also true with and each successive smaller unit of culture all the way down to a family. These smaller cultural units are extremely able to spring back into their original shape, so that family, tribe, community or sub cultural molarity can be completely straying from mainstream normative morality. At a time when boundaries are not clear and the globalisation characterised by intense interaction between cultures is increasingly important. Established between the communities, their relationship to one another, cultural and economic relations has been a confusing situation. Communities of different cultures that interact with each other more than to live in harmony with other communities can get to know their cultures. Culture is effective on communities that they have the level of civilisation, life style, material and spiritual elements and decisive as well as on the ethical perception it is one of the building blocks in the formation of communities. In this regard, in order to eliminate the negative effects of unethical behaviour is of great importance to understand the relationship between ethical perception and culture.

Ethics is one of the most important concepts of social reconciliation provide. Ethics considers the mutual benefit of interpersonal relationships, true false, showing the concept of the separation of the beautiful –ugly. In this sense, the development of individuals' perception of ethics cannot be considered independently of the culture to which they belong.

THE BIBLICAL WORLD VIEW SHOULD MAKE CHRISTIANS TO CHECK THEIR LIFE APPLICATION IF IT IS IN ACCORDANCE WITH CHRISTIANITY:

George Barna's research found that a very small percentage agree with the biblical world view. This means that to say there is something like biblical world view needs revisiting. His research also found that, although there was one Bible in every home, it is there to defend that I am a Christian, but the Bible is there in order for us to be able to know what the truth is and what is not. Although most Christians have Bibles in their homes, are they able to link the relationship that is there between the Bible and our life application? It appears they may stand parallel when it comes to what the Bible requires and how our lives are, people tend to live worldly lives as opposed to living Biblically. If we would view the world closely, how is it related to God, if we find out how it is related to God, where does a Christian fit in? If Jesus lived a sinless life and we want to emulate him, then we should try to re-examine our relationship with the world so that we are not in conflict with him. Yet Jesus prayed that we should be in the world as the salt of the world. It appears like we get carried away by the world and forget that, if Jesus conquered the world, we also have to do the same in order to represent him in this world. The Bible should always have a connection to reality in our lives; this means that a human being has got to live according to the teaching of the Bible. A human being was put on earth. It is becoming very fashionable that every home owns a Bible, but then it becomes meaningless if it is owned for the sake of defending ourselves that I am a Christian. Yet as inspired book it has to help us to make what is in it our life application. Therefore, biblical world view is to look at life in the world and link it with the life in the Bible as it is now. It is not only linking them, but to make them have harmony, because that is required of us. It is not enough to believe that we can be saved by self-purification, yet we may be saved by confession, that is linking our lives to the Creator. It is advisable to stay connected those who think differently might think that it is happening automatically. Let us not be resistant to the teaching of Christ, so that we get integrated to Christ and be true Christians. God created everything, in the end God said let us make man in our own image. After He had created a man He breathed his Spirit into the man, this means that spiritually, a man was made in the image of God. In other words, this means that the man is representing the kingdom of God on earth, which a man must take seriously, for he was given dominion over everything. This means that a man must treat every creation on earth with all the respect, because God created everything for a purpose.

MORAL TRUTHS SEEM TO APPLY TO EVERY CULTURE:

As there is a diversity of cultures, that means that the moral truth is valued differently. Moral truth in culture is something that is not invented by an individual; it is not something that an individual can sway to their side or to their way of thinking. It is something that is there to shape society, so in the end society will be how it should be. Statements should really conform to the reality than trying to make the world conform to statements. When we conform to the truth of the world, it is not a subjective truth but a moral truth. A moral truth stays the truth whether we like it or not, it will not change just to please an individual. Jesus was brought up in a Jewish culture, was his morality influenced by this culture, if it was not, what does that mean to us? Different cultures value thing differently, so that means that what may be valued with a certain culture as a moral truth may not be valued as a moral truth by the other culture. There is nothing like universal moral truth because of different values in different cultures.

THE BIBLICAL WORLDVIEW OF CHRISTIANITY AND THE CHURCH:

When Christians view the world, they have to view it basing their views with what the Bible says: *(1 John 2:15-18) (KJV)"Love neither the world nor the things that are in the world. If any man loves the world, the love of the Father is not in him. For all that is in the world, the lust of the flesh, and the lust of the eyes, and the pride of life is not of the Father, but is of the world. And the world will pass away, and the lusts will also pass away, but those who do the will of God will abide for ever. As the children of God, we have heard that there will come a time of anti-Christ, we can see now that there are forces that are antichrist and we know that these are the end times"* Worldliness is not limited to external behaviour, the people we associate with, the places we go, the activities we enjoy, worldliness is also internal, for it begins in the heart. It is characterised by three attitudes: 1 lust of the flesh-preoccupied with physical desires: 2 material things, "lust of the eyes" craving and accumulating wealth, and 3 pride of life-obsession with one's status of importance, when the devil tempted Eve (Genesis 3:6) (KJV) he tempted her in these areas. Also when Jesus was tempted in the wilderness, these were his three areas of attack, (Matthew 4:1-11) (KJV) God values self-control, a spirit of generosity, and humble service, you can have self-control and avoid "worldly pleasures" Jesus loved sinners and spent time with them, while maintaining the values of God's kingdom. What values are most important to you? Does your action reflect the values of the world or values of God? When we are very much attached to possessions, we must bear in mind that one day they will pass away. Yet one who does the will of God will live for ever. Let us know that our desires for the pleasures of this world will end, yet there is resurrection according to Jesus, this should give us courage. It has to be borne in mind that the Bible which we are referring to was inspired by God, so have to view the world basing on that basis so that when we about to wander away from it we are reminded so that we do not get astray. So if we would be looked at closely basing on the scripture, why then do we differ in our world view? Sometimes we have to be mindful so that we will not mix humanistic worldview with Biblical world view. Sometimes we get these things mixed up, and then in the end they tend to confuse us. Since there are so many denominations in Christianity, how they view the world now depends on the interpretation of those denominations, so Christians have no same definition of their world view depending on the denomination

THE CULTURAL MIND SET VERSUS CHRISTIANITY AND MAN:

(Dr Bruce Riley Ashford) Sometimes in life there appears to be some opposing factors between Christianity and culture. It appears each side would like to influence the other side. Sometimes you look at it; you see there is a tug of war between them. That is, between Church and culture.it appears up to this generation no one has sacrificed to bridge this gape that exist between them. From the look of it, you can see that no one side can be said it is winning, it would be said Christianity kills culture, but look at how Christianity is watered down, and look at how the church is mal-nourished these days. A task which does not require a single handed solution, but requires a spirit of togetherness, and asking for divine intervention. Infect it is a relationship that is required between them, other than opposing each other. What is required by Christianity is not fighting against those forces, but to try to win those forces to Christ. (John 17:20) (KJV) when Jesus prayed, He did not pray for Christians alone, but He wants those souls won to Him as well. He did not pray that the believers come out of the world, but to be the salt of the world. When Jesus said you are the salt of the earth, He wanted us to do what He commissioned us to do.

CHAPTER 19

CULTURAL TRADITIONS ARE, RITUALS AND CUSTOMS:

Culture sometimes deviates from God, and that sometimes culture is boastful, the culturalisms are supposed to realise that it is God who created culture. In (Acts Chapter 15) (KJV) and see how culture conflict with the will of God. Cultural traditions include events, rituals, and customs that a society shares. Mostly in funerals which run up to burials that is where most of cultural traditions are practised. Sometimes these practices deviate from God's will. These rituals vary from nation to nation. The problems that are faced in these traditions and rituals are that some nations or tribes will end up imposing them on other nations against their will. A tradition, belief or behaviour is passed down within a group or society with symbolic meaning or significance with origins in the past; these include holidays or socially meaningful clothes. These traditions persist and evolve for thousands of years, tradition means to transmit or to hand over, or to give for safekeeping. The problem that these traditions face is that they handed down orally, which means some of the values may be lost along the way. That is why some deviations are encountered along the way; if there are some amendments they are to please certain individuals. This means that there is still a lot of research and a lot of study to be made in this field, so that some individuals who might be influential may not impose their will on others. Some who believe in culture prefer to hold on to old traditions without taking into consideration that the changes might be meaningful sometimes. If changes are allowed to take place, these might be changes for the better, and would make the culture to go with the times.

CHAPTER 20

MULTICULTURALISM THE REALITY:

The world is fast becoming more and more multicultural, but even though they are becoming multicultural, they have not yet become fully integrated. The reason being, some cultures may be looking down upon other cultures, hence its failure to be a reality. The reason being that even they had a desire to go along with them; some cultures are still practising some primitive. Those who are practising that permittivity appear not to want to give them up. These range from; taking women as the property of men, UN able to make decisions on their own, deciding for young girls about their marriages, choosing partners for them. Although it appears multiculturalism is facing some problems here and there, it appears it's invading the world like a flame of fire, leaving it appearing like those countries that are accepting multiculturalism are becoming more and more advanced economically and technologically. It is viewed that it may be facing some difficulties, it appears and like those difficulties may be there for a near future.

God had a plan of salvation, even before the creation and the fall of man, because He said let us make man in our own image, and let him have dominion over all creation

THE EFFECT OF MULTI-CULTURALISM ON CHRISTIANITY:

Christianity did a lot in helping to end some of the deeds of darkness, which used to happen to society such as ending polygamy, human sacrifice infanticide and slavery, although things like slavery are still being practised, but they are being practised in a hidden and more tactful way. Christianity has uplifted the status of women that there is now a gender balance. Every nation has its own culture; there is only one Christianity, which means all these cultures have to find a common ground so they can be in one accord. Since we are coming with our different cultures to one common thing that means to say we have to be very cautious because we still have to get along with both. One thing has got to be looked into is that Christianity has done a lot to change people's lives but still people look at Christianity with some reservations, or are being hostile to the church. Christianity believes in the trinity. The work of the church is to follow the footsteps of Jesus, so the work of the church is to help people The church should behave in a moral way. Not all Christians must look to the government to look after the people Christians should be in the forefront to after the welfare of the people and the government will follow, in fact there should be some coordination. If there is a disagreement, something has gone wrong which must be looked into. The government and the church must work together to look after the people, with the church taking the lead. (Romans 5:8-9) (KJV) Jesus' mission on earth was to shade His blood on the cross to save everyone from their sin, Christians are following in the footsteps of Jesus, they must suffer for the good life of the people as Jesus did if we are to do His will. Christians must learn to respect cultural differences and to be able to accommodate them. Malt-culturalism must not surprise us because it has been there ever since. Think of the Samaritans, a mixed race and mixed cultures. Christianity and civilisation must help to take us from Dark Age and transform us from hostile cultures.

CHRISTIANITY HAS SUFFERED AS A RESULT OF MULTICULTURALISM:

It is a fact that when speaking of multiculturalism, we are speaking of so many different cultures that have come together having a common factor as wealth now being joined together to one culture of Christianity. But some cultures refuse completely to take Christianity; this is where Christianity is finding it difficult to proceed even with those that have taken Christianity as part of their culture. So, Christianity did not say abandon your culture, but only that there are some aspects which are anti-God that have to change. So it is not a matter of easy going, but requires some divine intervention. Divine intervention cannot come on its own accord without asking for it through prayers of those concerned. From the look of it, it appears, it is Christianity that is being diluted. If we look at history, it appears the rate at which Christianity spread compared to the rate it is spreading is less than it was spreading otherwise it would be said it is in a negative mode currently. It would be argued that Christianity is growing, but appears the growth could be selective, meaning that the growth could be noted in countries that are less multicultural. To those countries that are really multicultural, the growth is negative, so the fact remains that Christianity is in a negative growth.

Multiculturalism is opposed to missionary activity or attempts to morally reform culture, although Christianity strives to do things the way God likes them to be (not having a desire to kill culture) but some culturalisms do not want their culture touched, no matter they are to be reformed for the better of culture............. There was a fuss caused by the story about a child with some Christian heritage cared for by..........

TO ACCOMMODATE MULTI-CULTURALISM ACCEPT THAT THERE ARE DIFFERENT BELIEFS AND VALUES:

Christianity is being affected by multiculturalism, which means the way we look at Christianity versus culture must change if Christianity is to survive the test of times. Multiculturalism is affecting Christianity in that some cultures have never heard of Christianity or they did not want to accept it, hence to talk of Christianity to them they start saying it is imposed on us. Multiculturalism is opposed to missionary activity or attempts to morally reform culture. That is how it is opposed to Christianity. Christianity has to find ways and means to accommodate multiculturalism and convince them that there is a single creator who loves all regardless of their colour or creed. All cultures are equal in the eyes of the Lord. In those early days, missionary work used to spread quite rapidly, it appeared many cultures were responding to that, but it appears today missionary work seems to be on the decline. This has caused most cultures to shun Christianity, so where are we to start from? Maybe, since things have changed with the changing times, then Christianity has to change with the time. According to the "Great Commission" there is still need to spread the gospel, but how? In the end, Jesus said " I will be with you all ways". This means we have an assurance that we are not alone in that fight with forces of darkness. This is an encouraging promise for us not to be downhearted, but to soldier on.

CHAPTER 21

THERE IS A RELATIONSHIP BETWEEN BIBLICAL WORLDVIEW AND CHRISTIANITY:

(Christian Rethink) When dealing with Biblical world-view, we have to take our example from (Philippians chapter 2) (KJV) where, if we want to have good relations with Biblical world-view, we have to take our example from Christ Himself. Christ came into the world, although He was of a divine nature, He took a human nature. Even though He took a human nature, He managed to resist the temptations of the world. He was setting an example for us that we could also conquer the world if we follow His example. The example is that we do not have to take ourselves out of the world, in order to avert its sinful nature. At the great commission, instead Jesus is sending us into the world to mix with them, but the motive is not for us to be diluted by the world, but to win it to Christ. He is by the great commission sending us into the world with instructions in (John 4:35) (KJV), Jesus is teaching us that we should give excuses as to say my family is not yet ready to hear the word and accept it. Jesus is saying look around you and see that there are people who are ready to hear the word or to see your good works, so what are you waiting for? Work for the Lord while it is still day, for the time will come when we will not be able to, you have no one else to blame but yourself.

CHRISTIANITY MUST LEARN TO ACCEPT AND ACCOMMODATE CULTURAL DIVERSITY:

(Centre for Global Christianity and Mission) (Christianity and the World of Cultures) This multiculturalism which seems to be dividing the church should be looked into closely, because Christianity itself is multicultural because Christianity has not been made of one culture, but a diversity of cultures. For Christianity to be made malfunction by multiculturalism is what has to be looked into. Christians are urged to look into this subject positively because otherwise a division might arise where there is no division when it is only a matter of logistics. Since Christianity has become a world religion, this has threatened many forces of darkness which are now trying by all means to derail that religion. The biggest temptation for Christianity is to take some of the things in culture that are not Christian and bring them into Christianity, yet Christians are supposed to be the light of the world. (Matthew 5:14) Christians must show that light by the way we do things, the way we talk, the way we treat non-Christians, if anything, for the kingdom of heaven to come on earth is through Christians. What Christians need is good timing, where it is possible and necessary we should speak for Christ or to say that we should defend Christianity when it is required to do so. The world is waiting to see the light from us, so we should not hide that light, that is how Christ's light should shine for the world it has to be through us. Christianity had an influence in culture when it introduced missionary schooling, which had a big influence on the lives of the people. Also in most cases Christianity introduced rural hospitals which means it cared for the health of the people. The Jews believe that there is God, Christianity expanded it and believe that there is a Messiah who is Jesus Christ. When Jesus travelled among the Jewish nation during His life time on earth, He chose some twelve men whom He called disciples he taught them for three years wanting them to take up His mission when he finally leaves the earth. After Jesus had gone back to heaven these disciples took it up and started spreading His word as He had taught them. Now that the disciples have also gone, we are to take it up so that there is a continuity . That is how the Christian movement started and spread. Now two thousand years after Jesus had left this movement has grown to be the religion of the world, and it is still growing. This Christian movement believes in the Trinity, which means that they believe that there is God as Father, Jesus as the Messiah and the Holy Spirit; these three are in separable according to Christianity. These Christians say that as Jesus rose from the dead, so shall His followers also rise at the second coming of Christ. Although there are some religions which resend Christianity or to even say they hate Christianity, but their lives have been influenced by Christianity in one way or the other, with them not even taking any notice of it. There were some religions which were there long before Christianity, but they have now been overtaken by Christianity.

TODAY'S MAN HAS JUST INHERITED THE DISOBEYING, EVEN AT CREATION MAN DISOBEYED GOD:

The problem we face as Christians is that we are caught in between wanting to please our own brothers and sisters who might be following earthly practices taking these practices as our culture. They may be looking at us to go along with them. If we decide to obey God, then we might be labelled as uncooperative, yet if you decide to follow them, you might be going against the will of God.

If sin is disobedience to the will of God, why should a man disobey the will of God? If Adam disobeyed God, are we still disobeying God, and why?

THE TRUTH THAT IS THERE BETWEEN GOD AND MAN:

Sometimes the way to the Lord is like a person in a strange land. In a strange land, a navigator helps to give correct directions until you reach your destination. To ignore the navigator and pretend to know might lead to more confusion, and resulting into not reaching the intended destination.

When God created man, He did it out of love, as He did not just put him on earth as if He has put him in the wilderness without any guide. He put man on earth with the instruction manual, the Bible; because He knew that, it would be a confusing world. Man could not know what to follow, cultural practices or Christianity, the Bible clearly defines the relationship that is there between cultural practices and Christianity. Without a guide, it becomes more confusing, yet the way might not be that confusing when we are patient enough to follow guidance. (John 10:7-10) (KJV) Jesus states clearly that he is the way, which means if we follow him as guided by his word we will never go astray because it will mean following the way, the truth and the life. It requires to be followed closely by every individual, and in every situation of life, not half-heartedly. Life's journey needs to be followed without a divided mind, after a long perseverance, the way begins to be clear.

As He willingly made man in His own image, He willingly gives man directions, so that there is no confusion. Al His plans are not to harm a man nor to embarrass him, but to lead him gently to eternal life where there is everlasting joy. Since He put all His ways in the Bible, He expects us to follow His instructions. The Bible is a reliable Road map for our lives; the toughest challenges of life are made easy if we follow the navigator of life. God is very pleased if we obey His instructions, He is very willing to shower His blessings on those who obey His commandments. He does this through Jesus Christ the Saviour, who came to set an example, because he was both human and divine nature he feels the challenges of life as much as we feel, so he knows very well what challenges of life we might go through. His promises we know they are true when he said he would not leave us comfortless and that he would be with us in our everyday lives. We will never go wrong we can remember that he is always with us, and then we can always call on him when we find ourselves in a difficult situation. In any case we do not have to wait for a different situation, but to stay connected through a divine telephone which is always connected to the Trinity and all the heavenly beings. He can always renew our Spiritual lives as we live in it. Society must be transformed in order for it to do the will of God and be able to be accept in the kingdom of God:

Since God is Spirit, we must worship Him in Spirit and in truth. He is faithful to us; He is ready to listen to us when we talk to Him. We communicate with Him through Jesus Christ. Jesus gave us assurance that he would listen when we ask him what we want. Whenever we communicate with him, we must pre-empt ourselves knowing that he will use us the way he loves to use us for the good of his kingdom here on earth. (John 14:14) (KJV) says, "If you ask anything in my name I will do it". That means to say that we must have a relationship with him, meaning that what we ask from him must be for the furthering his kingdom on earth. We must avoid being selfish in our request. We must know that he examines our hearts. That is to say that we are asking him to purify us, when we are pure then we can ask him to give us the power to bring others to him, because that cannot be done by one who is unclean. Even though it is us who must forgive, we must ask him to give us the power to be able to forgive, otherwise we cannot do it on our own. If anything, we must have faith when we pray. When we pray, let us leave the answer to him because he is the one who knows his time frame. We know that he loves us much that he cannot fail to answer since he died on the cross to show us his love. Let us not forget to thank him for what he did to us. When Christians have a world view how do they react? The world is watching how Christianity is behaving by looking at Christians and they will decide whether to follow Christianity or not. So Christians are to be a show case for Christianity to society. (Paul Copan) (One place.com) accessed 15.12.2019.

Jesus Christ came to the world to set an example of how life should be lived here on earth. When he left, he gave us an assignment to continue where he left off, this means to say that we have resemble him in anything he did we must do it the same way as he did it, so it has to be an example to society. The main aim is to win them to Christ. Society is mostly in culture, but this does not mean that they are wrong, but that there are some aspects in culture that have to be corrected in order for them to be able to fit into Christianity. Christians are to be always faithful to what they do, because if they are not, what is the world going to copy. The aim of Christians has to be "faithful presence" sometimes Christians are tempted to want to change culture from within, but there is a danger of being swallowed by culture. If that happens, we forget that the original aim was to change society faithfully. Every step that a Christian takes is a measure that they arc measured with, which means their steps have to be in the right direction in order to attract many into Christianity.

CHAPTER 22

HOW CULTURE AND CHRISTIANITY ARE INTER WOVEN AND HOW THEY CAN BE ACCEPTED IN THE PRESENCE OF GOD:

Sometimes culture and Christianity seem to have a dividing line between them, because each one of them wants to dominate the other. Sometimes it appears the outside world is coming in full force (Revelations 3:11) (KJV), yet these two will always exist contemporarily.

Since culture is shared among a group of people, each member has to conform to the way the people in the group do things. Each member has to fit in or risk being classified as an outcast. Culture shapes people's personalities. People who are born and bred in the same culture share common personalities and something that displays their personalities reflects a person's tendencies, hardworking and to follow rules.

Beliefs and causes of diseases are influenced by culture. Degree of pain tolerance expected on some members of a group can influence how they seek medical help, (as an example, age or gender). Culture is not going into other's space but to learn how others are living so as to live in peace, finding ways of getting along. Culture sometimes deviates from God's will: Because of wanting to please others of the group (Romans 12:2) (KJV) If they are outclassed they do not conform to the pattern. The fact that Christianity was spiritually filled, led the Jews to start taking it as a rival religion, yet it was only their beliefs.

Cultures were there before Christianity, since then the people who were in culture are the very people who are taught what Christianity is.

WHAT PEOPLE DO IN CULTURE SHOWS WHAT THEY VALUE THE MOST IN LIFE:

People of different races and cultures are mixing more often than before; this is caused by the easy in travel. People are connected to each other more than before. There are so many cultures as there are so many geographical differences, religious/spiritual, sexual orientation general, family and gender. All these different cultures influence us in one way or another. We see the world through the cultural lens (is). Some of the cultures are learned, some are inherited: some cultures want to dominate other cultures depending on the situation, as an example:

> .*Corporate culture dominates over national culture*
> .*National culture dominates over religious culture*
> .*Religious culture dominates over sexual orientation*
> .*Generational culture dominates over gender culture.*

A number of aspects influence the way we interact with other people, and various communication styles: They influence how we conduct our work:

Our behaviour and style:
Our use of language:
How we solve challenges, problems, and conflicts:
How we negotiate, and
How we go about creating relationships.

Values and beliefs are learnt in a national culture and they may be unconscious. You may not be aware of your values and beliefs until you are confronted by someone different.

MEDIEVAL ATTITUDE TOWARDS CHRISTIANITY:

Sin in Christianity teaching, consists of disobedience to the known will of God. The first example of sin described in the Bible comes in the story of Adam and Eve, who were placed by God in the Garden of Eden. They chose to disobey God, and as a result, were expelled from His presence and condemned to live in a harsh and inhospitable world. The medieval church inherited some political powers which were invested in the Pope; most of the church's powers were obeyed. There was some stability in the church those days that the people relied on them. Currently politics has taken away most of the church's powers, for example, churches used to run schools and hospitals, which is no more the case these days.

The main way in which humanism contradicted medieval attitudes towards Christianity was that it literally put emphasis back on human themselves, and it spoke to the humanity and importance of the individual, as opposed to the individual being simply a servant of God.

The key aspects of middle Ages were the emphasis on authority –people would believe what they were told against the evidence of their own eyes.

THERE HAS TO BE SOME RELATIONSHIP BETWEEN HUMANITY AND CHRISTIANITY.

(bbc.co.uk) (accessed 17 September 2020) Christians believe that human life is sacred and it is God given this theory could be beyond any doubt, because God created man in His image. There is some debate between those who represent humanity and those who represent Christianity in order to find common ground. The common ground is that they are all humans, and that the environment can affect them all.

If culture is a way of life, and the Lord said, let us make man in our own image, then there has to be some relationship between God and culture.

Genesis 1:26 There is good relationship between God and man in that God created everything on earth and gave man dominion over them. Man never created anything, but to be made in charge of His creation is a great honour which a man should not under estimate. Since when God looked at the creation He said it was good, hence, man must maintain that goodness. There is an agreement between God and man, God gives a man an assignment a man has to perform his assignment and to give an account in the end. This is an agreement we must take seriously after God did his own job he handed it to man in good faith, God expects a man to do his part and honour the agreement. The author is pleading with the reader to consider that when someone requests you to look after His possession you have to be responsible for you will have to give an account when the owner comes. When God created a man He already had a plan of salvation. When it is said, Go loved the world that He gave His only son, it did not start there but at creation. Our beliefs habits ideas and customs must be perfect in the presents of God that although they represent our culture they must be acceptable to the creator. God would like us to treat one another as equals for we were all created in the image of God so we are all the children of one Father, who loves us. God loves every one of us He prepared salvation for everyone, but we have to take this with caution because it is not everyone one who says Lord who will enter the kingdom. Salvation is there but it us who will distance ourselves from the salvation. Let us take our example from the Garden of Eden, the man was not chased from the garden but he went into hiding.

CHAPTER 23

THE WORK OF THE CHURCH IS TO GUIDE THE PEOPLE INTO GOOD BEHAVIOUR:

As there is required an individual to worship, there is also need for collective worship. As the government is there to look after the people physically, and ensure that, their physical needs are met. So does the church look after the spiritual needs of the people, the church make sure that people are not starved spiritually? Today the human knowledge is acquired through the work of the church, whether people believe in it or not, the fact still remains that most of the knowledge today is through the work of the church (Daniel 12:4) (KJV) It would be better if governments would work together, for the common good. Governments want peace in the country, and the church also wants peace. Their approaches are different, governments believe in punishing if it wants to discipline it subjects, the church believes in teaching and guiding the people in a friendly manner. Both their methods are good that is why we say they must find common ground because their goal is the same only the approach.

THERE IS A RELATIONSHIP BETWEEN HUMAN AND CULTURE:

(https://blog.faithlife.com) (Accessed 27.05.2020) There is a tug-of-war between cultures and Christianity in that culture is trying to make Christianity come to its side. Christianity is saying, yes culture is a way of life, but let it not be culture without faith, because culture has to have some faith in the Creator, then that can be a starting point of our relationship. When God said let us make man in our own image, that means there has to some relationship between God and man. Culture should not try to live in isolation of faith that means it is disconnecting itself from its creator. The problem we are faced with is not to try to separate the two, but to try to join them already from the creation it has shown that they are in separable, but then how are we going to make them work together in harmony. Culture includes; knowledge, belief, art, law, morals, and habits. The other problem faced by culture is that it is transmitted from one generation to the next generation verbally, so some will try to bend it in such a way that it suits their needs, and their way of life. Culture is not something that an individual cannot say I want it or I do not want it, because it something that is shared among a certain group, if you say I do not want it, you could be an outcast. Christianity and Judaism have faith in God, so if culture says I have faith in culture only, but man was created in the image of God and culture is not separated from man who was created in the image of God.

CULTURE PLAY A ROLE IN MAKING PEOPLE CLOSER TO THE GOSPEL BECAUSE IT IS A SHAPER OF PERSONALITY, WHICH IN TURN WILL SHAPE OUR CHRISTIANITY:

Morality must be based on absolute truths, but absolute truth may be difficult to define because it may depend on what that society values, and what that society calls moral truths. This may be true only where we have universal moral standards that might apply to every culture. Morality is a restraint on natural human behaviour; *how is morality a restraint to natural human behaviour? (Check)* morality should be a reflection of God's character. Before we even go anywhere, the fact that God created us in His own image shows us that He loves us, (one good turn deserves another) so we have to return that love by loving Him as our creator and saviour. But human nature and that these truths are determined by the fact of our creation by God as being designed for relationships with God and one another. If we have sinned, we have someone who intercedes for us. Furthermore we have claimed that a reliable definitive expression of these absolute moral truths is to be found uniquely in the Christian revelation preserved in the Bible. *What truth is preserved in the Bible?* A moral truth cannot apply to every culture, because different cultures have different cultural values, so absolute truths will apply differently, not as a blanket. All this talk of moral absolutes based on absolute truths is, to use the usual expression, politically incorrect. Those who dare to suggest that there are absolute truths that apply to all people in all cultures are usually deemed narrow minded and culturally imperialistic. The charge is made even more vehemently when the absolutes, which are held, find their normative expression within the context of the Biblical worldview. Belief in Jesus Christ as the only way to God is associated by all non-Christians and even many within the Christian Church today, with "Eurocentrism" a cultural mind-set that exalts the perspectives and achievements of male white Europeans (and their dependents in North-America) at the expense of other cultures and traditions. As Islam and the Eastern Religions have come into greater cultural prominence and acceptance in the West, belief in absolute truth of the religious and moral teachings of Christianity is now commonly viewed as arrogant, intolerant, and unrealistic in today's pluralistic society.

How shall we respond to this increasingly common sentiment? How can we call on all people to submit to Jesus Christ as Lord and Saviour to embrace the faith and values of Christianity in a society zealous for cultural diversity?

Christ was always truthful, as He is always truthful, by following Him, you are absolute truth, but do not claim others untruthful. Just stick to your truthfulness as a follower of Christ. As Christ was always truthful, by following Him, we are also following absolute truth, but we should not claim others are untruthful. We must stick to our faith as followers of Christ.

HOW DO CULTURE AND CHRISTIANITY COMPLEMENT EACH OTHER?

Christianity watches culture closely because sometimes culture is corrupted by sin, because there are so many different cultures, which will mean that there are so many different values in culture. Unlike Christians who values the same, Christianity does want a single culture to dominate the others

Christians do not get surprised when there is multiculturalism. The fact that there are so many cultures in Christianity today has made it to be like this, some nationalities might accept one aspect of culture into Christianity while the other nationalities do not.

CHAPTER 24

HOW BELIEVING JEWS BECAME CHRISTIANS:

(Ruth Rosen) (Jewish and Christian) (jewsforjesus.org) it was not a simple matter to convert from Judaism to Christianity because Jews believed that they were the chosen people. For them to convert to a religion that includes gentiles was like being degraded, so they could not take it. Even to this day, it is still difficult to convince people that Jesus is for all nations. He generously provided us with His grace and mercy. It is up to us to accept or reject His grace. He poured His Holy Spirit on then gentiles without first going through the Jewish culture as required by the Jews. They had set a precondition that they to converting to Judaism, it was mostly the work of the Holy Spirit which revealed to some Jews that God was for all the people, the Holy Spirit revealed to them that although they were first chosen, they were to be the light to the gentiles. There were some who did not have the revelation remained in believing in Judaism, that is why they were divided up to this date.

CONSERVATIVE JUDAISM'S BEGINNINGS:

(Masorti Judaism) is a Conservative Judaism, which regards the authority of Jewish law and tradition as emanating primarily from the ascent of the people and the community and the generations, more than from divine revelation. That is, we should always be asking the Lord to give us a revelation that we do not end up giving the Glory to the people, something that was supposed to go to the creator. Conservative Judaism views Jewish,

(Halakha) as both binding and subject to historical development. What should be binding in our lives is the Holy Scripture. Our life application has to be modelled on Him who lost His life on Calvary for you and me. We must lead a life of obedience; a life of being guided by His divine power which will make our relationship with Him a sound relationship. The Conservative (rabbinate) employ modern historical and critical research rather than only traditional method and sources, and lands great weight on its constituency, when determining its stance on matters of practice. The movement considers its approach as authentic and most appropriate continuation of (halakhic) discourse, maintaining both fealty to receive forms and flexibility in their interpretation. It also eschews strict (Theological) definitions, lacking consensus in matters of faith and allowing great pluralism. Other than coming to Him in a boastful way, we should humble ourselves, and then He is the one who will exalt us not ourselves, Romans 9:26. The problem we face as Christians today could be of superiority. Yet the Lord is looking for those who humble themselves; those who pre-empty themselves so that He can fill them with the Holy Spirit. The problem we might be facing as Christians of today is that of being carried away and start thinking that I was created superior than others,(Acts 15:1-31) (KJV). (Hosea 1:10) (KJV) and (Hosea 2:23) (KJV), are prophesies of the coming of the gentiles to Christianity. Jews were not happy, but they forgot that they should rely on divine revelation, but were relying more on themselves. We are also being reminded here not to rely heavily on our cultural things than on divine guidance. Like in Romans 9:26 Paul is reminding us that when we do our cultural things let us not forget to link them to Christ for guidance. Conservative Judaism had drifted from the original without them knowing it; they started relying on the ascent of the people than on divine guidance. The (rabbinate) although they were not relying on the old way of doing things, but were applying new techniques, they still relied on their own knowledge than on divine guidance. It has to be bone in mind that the promise that was made to Abraham, was made to him because of his faith, so those who are faithful, will become the children of Abraham by faith, hence biological connection should not be mixed with faith connection. Where these rabbinates were out of touch was that they believed that for everyone to be accepted by God, they had to be converted to Judaism first, yet gentiles received the

Holy Spirit without first converting to Judaism. Genesis 6:5 man chose sin and death instead of building relationship with God. Before the coming of Jesus, Jewish males used to have a model prayer of saying "God I thank you because I am not a gentile, I am not a slave or a woman" by the coming of Jesus, all that was abolished that is why when gentiles started coming into Christianity, the Jews were trying to resist it. In Christ all believers are one, that is why even to this day people are insisting that there should always be a gender balance, something of which even to this day some are still trying to resist it. This is against what Jesus went on the cross for, He went on the cross to liberate women, gentiles and slaves. Let us ask the Lord to give us courage to be able to accommodate the changes that were brought about by Jesus. May our dear Lord help us to appreciate that in the eyes of God we are one. As we try to resist, we are putting a burden on ourselves, for Jesus never changes, it is us who have to change. Also look at the covenant that was made with Abraham, it was meant for every person in the world not a selected ones, (Galatians 3:28) (KJV). There is neither Jew nor gentile, (Acts 17:15-34) (KJV) engage culture with respect. (Matthew 6:19-20) (KJV): In the new covenant Jesus is teaching about total surrender to the will of the Lord not half-heartedly by having total commitment you will be laying your treasures in heaven. (Exodus 20:2-3) (KJV),(1 Corinthians 6:19-20) (KJV),(1 Thessalonians) (KJV), about controlling our bodies.

(FROM THOMPSON MANDAZA: 07.03.2018)

Follow the story of Jesus and the Samaritan woman closely and it will answer the question of; "Does Christianity kill Culture?" Here the different cultures of Jews and Samaritans have been made into one by Christianity and perfected. In the end they were all into one culture which Jesus does not hastate to say it is a perfect culture.

There is also need to look at various stories Told by Jesus Himself during His ministry in which he referred to the practices by Pharisees and Sadducees as the preservers of culture who demanded action from others which themselves could not do. Also of importance, the story of the Samaritan woman who met Jesus at the well, how he defended their practice in reference to what the Jews expected of them. The conclusion of this story is interesting, where the whole community turns to God after Jesus had shown them the way. This is a typical example of cultural cleansing.

JOHN CHAPTER 4 JESUS AND THE SAMARITAN WOMAN:

The Samaritan woman broke the cultural barrier; she overcame the culture of the Jews and the Samaritans for women not to be allowed to speak to men in public. This barrier made the Samaritans not to associate with Jews. She broke the barrier of being a known sinner. Her boldness was in contrast to the role in which women were frequently placed culturally. Her boldness made a difference. She represented all women in her boldness.

There are some examples of Jesus with women in the Gospel of John, Jesus associated with some other women, like Mary the mother of Jesus, Mary Magdalen and Martha. Jesus might have done this on purpose in order to break the cultural barriers that existed against women during his ministry. Women typically maintained their social role, but during Jesus' ministry, they were exalted from that time onwards. The woman at the well was an example of "good soil" ready to hear the testimony of the Messiah, there is a contrast between this story and that of Nicodimus. (Thompson Mandaza ends)

The tension between the Jews and the Samaritans was such that, when the Samaritans offered to help in the rebuilding of the Temple of Jerusalem, the Jews refused, the Samaritans then decided to build their own temple at Mount Gerizim, the Jews destroyed it, that was some 150 years before Christ. Whenever there was going to be any marriage between the Jew and the Samaritan, the marriage was refused. Therefore, it is not surprising when a Samaritan woman says to Jesus, why you ask for water from the Samaritan woman.

The Samaritan culture had come about like this: the Assyrians raided the Northern kingdom, and they were conquered. The Assyrians feared the nation they had conquered might one day regroup and revolt. So all the able boded were sent into exile to Babylon and Assyria and some other countries. They brought in the colonists from Assyria, who caused inter marriage; hence the nation became a half cast nation. The tension between the Jewish culture and the Samaritan culture, back dates to the twelve sons of Jacob, (Genesis 37:3-4) (KJV) Joseph's brothers hated their brother so bad that they decided to end his life when God intervened and saved Joseph's life who later saved his brothers' and family's lives from a severe famine when Joseph was in charge in Egypt. When they came out of Egypt to the Promised Land, and after the reigns of King David and his son Solomon, there was a split of the whole nation because of taxation. There were two nations, one settled in the North and called themselves Israel, and their capital being Samaria, while the other half remained in the South, and were called Juda. The Northern kingdom was unfortunate to have been raided by the Assyrians. While they were under the Assyrian rule, the Assyrians feared that the Israelites might revolt. That is the reason why they sent all the young men into exile because they wanted to keep the peace. When the Assyrians brought in the colonists, they brought with them their pagan gods and mixed them with the God of Israel, this angered the Jews even more. Because of the intermarriage, the race became a mixed race which was hated by the Jews more than they hated the gentiles. It became one of the Jewish cultures to say that no one should have any dealings with the Samaritans.

Jesus being of the Jewish culture, he had to abide by the Jewish culture, and follow the Jewish culture, and treat the Samaritans as unholy. But Jesus being of two natures, wholly human and wholly spiritual, he would not get instructions from humans. There are two cultures here; the Jews are following their culture not associate with Samaritans (which they thought they were doing God a service). Jesus was following a Spiritual culture to be a friend of sinners. Jesus is on a mission, he came here to seek the lost sheep. Jesus was trying to make them see that their culture was different from the Christian culture, when he had to show them by means of a parable of the Good Samaritan. The parable showed them that a Jew was abandoned by fellow Jews only to be helped by a Samaritan.

THE SAMARITAN CULTURE TOWARDS CHRISTIANITY OR GOD:

Jesus was a great teacher who would teach thousands of people at once, but at the same time Jesus was a great one- one teacher, an example was his conversation with the Samaritan woman at the well. The Samaritans belong originally to the tribe of Ephraim and Manasseh and also to the tribe of Benjamin. They say from the 1960s, this tribe of Benjamin is instinct. Tainted by the colonists from Assyria and Babylon they became a mixed race, who were very hated by the Jews, but even though to this date, the Samaritanism is more inclined to Judaism and their religion still resembles Judaism.

The reason why Jesus had to go through Samaria was that even to this day there is still some confusion as to which is the holy place of worship, mount Gerizim or Jerusalem. Yet Jesus said to the Samaritan woman, the place of worship is not what matters, but what matters is to worship God in truth and in Spirit.

Once a large community, the Samaritan population appears to be shrinking as a result of the conversion to Christianity of the Byzantium Empire, Islam and Judaism. As per the statistics of January 1 of 2017, the population of pure Samaritans had dwindled to 796; some are still having a conversion to Judaism because of inter marriage. Although they still want to maintain their pure Samaritanism. To this day the wars in the Middle East are still having an effect on this population. Look at the church history, how the culture of the Jews affected their relationship with God, yet it was clear that their practices were anti-God. Let us also look at the early Christian movement. The Gospel of John and Revelations are critical references as they show how the Johannine community of these early days tried to evade persecution in order to preserve Christianity. The major issue here was misconception that Christianity could destroy their culture, (as is still happening today).

We may further look at how the Israelites got various punishments after defying God by embarking on unholy practices. *What practices did they do which were unholy, and what punishment did they get?* However, never the less, God continued to save them. Stories in Exodus, Leviticus, and Deuteronomy could be perfect examples of cultural deviation from God's way.(check)

THE EARLY CHURCH WAS AFFECTED BY CULTURE:

(The True Church History, rcg.org) Jesus said to Peter, "On you I will build my Church" How was He going to build it, where the church now? Since 2000 years ago, people are still starting new churches expecting that they are starting the right one. Christian culture means the culture practised by Christianity, at the end of the 4th century Christianity became the official language of the Roman Empire. The reason why there is what is called human rights, the world over, is following the concept that God said "Let us make man in our own image." In those early ages, women were regarded as man's property. The church is for human rights, it had to change that, also the church has been handling things like social services, schools, medical care, art, culture and philosophy. Also even when politicians were going astray they let them know that the people belong to God and are to be treated as human beings. This is not history, but it appears the church is still taking a leading role in education and politics.

Jesus was always conflicting with the Pharisees and Sadducees on how they wanted their culture observed.

Some kind of divine revelation has to be asked for, in order to be able to understand why Jesus was called king of the Jews when the Jews were under the Roman rule. This means that His kingdom is a heavenly kingdom and not an earthly one. But He was never understood. This book is pleading with the reader, to ask for a revelation because this generation must avoid the same pitfall like that generation. That generation could not understand, because they could not understand His kingship. This led them to plot His crucifixion. The Roman government thought that one day He was going to lead soldiers and bring down their empire, all this was from their misunderstanding. The Jews on the other hand thought that He was killing their culture and the Law of Moses.

HOW WE WANT CULTURE TO BE OBSERVED TODAY:

When faced with multi culturalism these days it is better to cast your eyes broadly and see what is happening worldwide? Good communication skills might bridge the gap, look broadly on traditional holidays, festivals food and many others. Good listening skills in order to know what are the requirements of those under you or below you. Allow social connections and social activities.www.deakinco.com (accessed 20.9.2020) "Cultural awareness is sensitivity to the similarities and differences that exist between two different cultures and the use of this sensitivity in effective communication with members of another cultural group". When communicating with different cultures, be always aware and alert in order to avoid bad or poor decisions. To be always aware helps us to have good decisions, which will help to keep good relationship and harmony? Learn to accommodate cultural differences this will help us to avoid stereotyping, if you respect other people's cultures that will help you tolerate what others do. Try to make the environment enjoyable to everyone so that everybody enjoys being there. Please note that everyone value his or her culture. So try to respect what they value, hence learn to respect cultural differences.

THE PHARISEES:

The Pharisees were those who observed God's law to every detail: They believed that the kingdom of God would come when the people observed the law perfectly. They hated the Romans, and were very spiritual people, but not very practical. They hated the Romans, but the only strategy they proposed to overcome them was to observe all the commandments to the letter. This kind of attitude did not make the Romans give up their empire. The Pharisees shared the problem and difficulties of the poor and oppressed people, but did not do anything to solve their tragic social situation.

The land owners had taken away most of the land of Galilee, the richest region, and the poor had nothing to eat. That is why some of the people went to the mountains and joined bands of thieves. In that situation, the Pharisees used to say, let us be good and follow the law, and then God will solve the other problems of life. This was the attitude of the Pharisees: spiritual people, very religious, but no practical commitment to solve the social problems of simple people. These were the spiritual guides of the people! They were not rich: many had a normal job, and propose themselves as models to imitate by the simple people of Galilee if they wanted to be perfect. They consider themselves to be superior to others. That is why Jesus accused them of being "hypocrites".

THE SADDUCEES AND THEIR BELIEF:

The Sadducees had the political and economic power. Members of the rich families both civil and religious formed this party. They were not interested in the kingdom of God or in the coming of the Messiah. Their only worry was to keep their social status and have their respect of the Romans. Therefore, every change in society was dangerous in their eyes, and did not doubt in using violent means against their compatriots when they provoked rebellions, revolts, or disturbed the peace somewhere.

Obviously, the simple people did not connect with them, but still respected them because they gave the impression of observing the law. They had the majority in the Sanhedrin (council) which helped them to impose their ideology, based on the political and economic interest of the Romans. Therefore, the people could not see any way out of their miserable situation. If they needed courage to fight the Romans, they needed more to confront the political and religious authorities. This group also opposed the Pharisees.

THE ZEALOTS:

The Zealots (=Zealous), like their name indicates, was a party formed by observant and devout Jews who wanted to accelerate the coming of the kingdom of God by fighting the Romans with the sword.

In the mountains of Galilee, they used the guerrilla strategy to fight the Romans. In Jerusalem during the main feasts, they would hide among the crowds to kill Roman soldiers and also Jews accused of collaborating with Romans.. To do that, they used a short curved knife called "sisca" that could be hidden easily under the clothes. For them, it was a "holy war" against the invaders. This was started by human hands, but God would intervene through the Messiah to finish it and liberating them from slavery of the Romans and corrupted Jews in the government. Many simple people sympathised with them because they offered a way out to change this situation.

The Zealots belonged to the lowest class, the simple and oppressed people. Apart from the "holy war", they proposed a social revolution for improving the life of the poor. That is why during the war, they burnt the archives with people's debts which were in Jerusalem. They also proposed a political revolution, substituting authorities who were corrupted or collaborated with the Romans. With others worried about the deeds of the simple people.

THE ESSENES:

The group of Essenes does not appear in the New Testament. They left the public society and went to the desert of Qumran to expand their life in prayer and religious meditation. This movement had no political ideology and refused any public activities in the country. They believed that the present situation of Roman oppression was caused by their unfaithfulness to God's law. That is why they returned to the desert and broke up with political and religious institutions of Israel: the temple, the priests the authorities.

They were convinced that the only remedy to their suffering was returning to the strict observation of law, the life of prayer, and the study of the Torah. They called themselves "the chosen ones" the true people of Israel who will inherit God's promises. They had a good internal organisation and several ceremonies and rituals. They lived an ascetic life and many of them did not marry voluntarily (celibate). The belief of the Essanes that the Holy war meant the coming down of the Messiah to finish it for it them, seems to have been carried down and inherited currently.

Actively. They wrote an essay about it where it is said that the Messiah would lead the army, play the trumpets, and win over the gentiles and oppressors. It was the dream of the oppressed people of Israel.

SCRIBES:

Scribes (1906 Jewish Encyclopaedia) were a board of teachers who were used to interpret the law to the people, their organisation beginning with Ezra, who was their chief, ending with Simeon the Just. The original meaning of the Hebrew word "Soferim" was "people who know how to write": and therefore the Royal Officials who were occupied in recording in the archives the preceding of each day were called "scribes", but as the art of writing was known only to the intelligent, the term "scribe" became synymous with "wise men". Later in the time of Ezra, the term's designation was applied to the body of teachers who, as stated above, interpreted the law to the people. Ezra himself is styled "a ready scribe in the Law of Moses". Indeed he might be so correctly called, for two reasons, in as much as he could write or copy the law and at the same time was an interpreter of it. The Rabbis however, deriving from "to count" and interpret the term "Soferim" to mean those who count the letters of the Torah or those who classify its contents and count the number of laws and or objects are belonging in each group. We have an example of five classes of the people that are exempt from the heave offering, four chief causes of the damage, thirty-nine chief works that are forbidden on Sabbath day etc. This may be the only interpretation of the "Soferim". It is evident that the works of these scribes were the first teachers of the Torah and founders of the oral law. The activities of the scribes began with the cessation of that of the prophets after the Israelites who came back from Babylon who had turned their hearts to God. There was a greater need of men to instruct the people, and assist them in obtaining a clear understanding of the law. "Zacharias Frankel" identifies this body of teachers with the "men of Great Synagogue" of whom Simeon the Just was the last member. (If this identification is correct) the organisation of scribes lasted from the time of Ezra till the conquest of Palestine by Alexander the Great, a period of 200 (two hundred) years. It must be said, however, that the term "Soferim" was sometimes used, particularly, in the post Maccabean time to describe teachers generally. Thus Moses and Aaron are styled as the "Soferim of Israel". As a general rule, the term refers to the body of teachers, the first of whom was Ezra and the last was Simeon the Just. It appears as if after Simeon, the teachers were generally styled "elders", and later "the wise ones". Later, the activities of the scribes were manifold, yet the main activity was to teach the Torah to the Jewish masses and to the Jewish youth in particular. It was they who established schools and they were particularly enjoined to increase the number of pupils. Therefore, they read the books in the law of God distinctly, and give the sense, and caused them to understand the reading. From the time of Ezra, however, the scribes occupied themselves also with plans for raising Judaism to a higher intellectual plane. They were consequently, in reviving the use of Hebrew, which had been largely forgotten during the exile in Babylon, and in giving it more graceful and suitable script. There were two kinds of professional scribes: the ones who were engaged in the transcript of the Pentateuch scroll and ones who acted as notaries public and court secretary.

The Jewish Scribes used the following rules and procedures while creating copies of the Torah and eventually other books in the Tanakh. They could only use clean animal skins, both to write on and even to bind manuscripts. The scribes had knowledge of the law and could draft legal documents (contracts for marriage, divorce, loans, inheritance, mortgages, the sale of land and the others). According to Mark's gospel, they were Jesus' main adversaries. Because they had studied the law, they used to confront Jesus the same as the Pharisees.

JESUS CHALLENGES THE PHARISEES ABOUT THEIR CULTURES:

(Matthew 15:1-20) (KJV) Even the present day, laws might be bent to suit those who will be ruling that time. Sometimes these changes might be slight changes at a time, as time goes, if you look back and reflect you will note that you have drifted for a long distance. From the time of the Law of Moses to the time of Jesus the law of Moses was completely changed, but they still thought that they were still within the law, until Jesus reminded them that they had drifted. The laws were so changed that they were exalting just a few forgetting the majority. When He challenged them, they started plotting Him because He had exposed their weaknesses. From this time on, they were asking Him questions that would lead them to His arrest, but Jesus' time was not yet. One that Jesus pointed out to the Pharisees was that some of them were blindly following. One major thing that made the Pharisees and Sadducees different was that the Sadducees were supportive of the Roman Government, which according to the Pharisees was oppressing the people.

PHARISEES AND SADDUCEES WERE PRESERVERS OF THEIR CULTURE:

Pharisees and Sadducees were both prominent Jewish sects who existed during Christ's time were both inclined to the law of Mosses and both opposed to the teaching of Jesus. They plotted the death of Jesus because both (Pharisees and Sadducees) their deeds were exposed by Jesus, how they disagreed with Jesus was that the Pharisees disagreed with Him when He healed on a Sabbath, they said it was breaking the law. The Sadducees disagreed with Jesus when He refused them to take their dead brother's wife. They said the Law of Moses allowed them to take their brother's wife to make seed for him. The Pharisees also accused Him for eating with sinners, but He answered them that one who is well does not need physician. The Sadducees disagreed with Jesus when He says there will be the resurrection of the dead while they say there is no resurrection of the dead.

THE JEWISH EXPECTATION OF THE SAMARITANS WAS:

The Northern kingdom when they were raided by the Assyrians most of the able boded were exiled and the colonisers brought in Assyrians which caused a lot of inter marriage which brought a mixed race, the Samaritans. The Jews hated this race. There was no relationship between the Jew and the Samaritans. The Samaritans were a race, which came out of all kinds of people. They were Israelites who were not exiled when the Northern Kingdom was destroyed in 722 BC. Other various different nationalities that the Assyrians had brought in from other conquered nations. The Samaritans could make pilgrimage to mount Gerizim because it was their holy place. When Jesus spoke to a Samaritan woman at the well, she said, "How is it you a Jewish man ask for a drink from me a Samaritan woman?"(Jews do not share things in common with Samaritan) That is the reason why today the story of the Good Samaritan is popular because he broke the barrier that was there between the Samaritans and the Jews.

THE SAMARITAN CULTURE TOWARDS CHRISTIANITY OR GOD:

Even during the time of Jesus, the Samaritan still believed that the place of worship was very important. Their belief was based on the Pentateuch; to them they believed it to be the true religion of the ancient Israelites before the Babylonian captivity. Those who remained in the land of Israel kept (preserved) this belief as original the first five books of the bible "Pentateuch", these were opposed to Judaism. Their religion is the Samaritanism; this religion believes in the Torah, they believed that they were following the original, which was not a changed Torah, which was different to the one used by the Jews. Both Jews and Samaritans when they were being converted to Christianity, a man called Prochorus played an important role, in developing early Christianity among Jews and Samaritan, who were being converted to Christianity. (Luke 9; 51-56) (KJV) Jesus was not welcome in Samaria. When Jesus wanted to go to Jerusalem, He wanted to pass through Samaria. He sent James and John to prepare, but the Samaritans refused to permit them to prepare for Jesus' passing through. The disciples were angry and asked Jesus to let them call fire from heaven to come down and consume them. Jesus rebuked the disciples and said; the Son of man did not come to destroy but to heal. This is a lesson to us that no matter what the word does against us we must always follow Jesus 'example.

THE SAMARITAN COMMUNITY AFTER BELIEVING IN JESUS:

Samaritans believe Judaism and the Jewish Torah have been corrupted by time and no longer served the duties God mandated in Mount Sinai. Samaritans were a nation of mixed races of the Northern kingdom, when the Northern kingdom was destroyed in 722BC of various different nationalities whom the Assyrians had resettled in the area. After the story of the Good Samaritan, they are now associated with doing well. Samaria also called Sebastes, modern Sebastian, and ancient town in central Palestine. It is located on a hill northwest of Nablus in the West Bank territory under Israel administration since 1967.

THE SAMARITAN CULTURE AFTER BELIEVING IN JESUS:

The purpose of Jesus meeting the Samaritan woman at the well was to bridge the gap that existed between the Jews and the Samaritans. Before that, there was a nasty tension between the two nations, when the tension was raging; no one of the Jews was allowed to pass through Samaria. That means when Jesus chose to pass through Samaria, He did it for a purpose, (John 4:1-4) (KJV). There was a conversation (exchange) between Jesus and this (strange) Samaritan woman, the broke so many barriers here, The barrier that a Jew cannot pass through Samaria, a barrier that a Jew cannot speak to a Samaritan, a barrier that a woman is not allowed to speak to a man in public, a Samaritan woman to a Jewish man for that matter, (John 4:5-26) (KJV). With the disciples not knowing what is going on Christ Jesus was very busy making His schedule, making things to happen at the time they were supposed to happen, He could make one thing to build the other. For example, going through Samaria, talking to a Samaritan woman, (John 11:34-44) (KJV) the raising of Lazarus. He would do these purposely knowing that this would build tension with the Jews, hence working towards His crucifixion. Yet all these things were planned when He was sent on a mission on earth that is why on the cross He said He had accomplished His mission. (Matthew 27:18) (KJV) when Jesus was brought before Pilate, he even found that there was nothing specific, but only that it was envy.

JESUS DISCUSSED JEWISH LAW WITH THE PHARISEES BECAUSE THEY WERE ADDING THEIR OWN:

(Matthew 23:23-39) (KJV), when Jesus said he had not come to abolish the law, but to fulfil it, he meant that, people should practise what they preach. They were putting burdens on others of the things they could not do themselves. Paul also refers to it in (Acts chapter 15:10-11) (KJV), when he says do not put a yoke on the shoulders of disciples, of which they themselves could not bear. Jesus wants us to go deeper in what we do so that we do not blindly lead others to do the wrong thing.

Always weigh the truth that is there between man and God. What he meant was that the kingdom of God must be revealed on earth through us. (Mark 7:5-7) (KJV) is a reflection of (Isaiah 29:13) (KJV), trying to make us come away from honouring the Lord with our lips, not meaning it whole heartedly, let us say what we really mean. Let us not appear clean outwardly. When are we going to leave doing things to be seen by men? Jesus is blaming in totality, though he was against their deeds, there were some outstanding characters like Nicodimus and Joseph of Arimathea who were members of the Sanhedrin, yet, inside them they knew Jesus was right, and that he really represented the kingdom of God. Jesus told them to desist from pronouncing the law from corners of streets, wanting to be seen by men that they knew the laws. Yet, Jesus said, let it come from deep down your heart. When we say, thy kingdom come, we are praying for the Lord to transform us in such a way that, the way we talk, walk, and do our work, interact with others should represent the kingdom here on earth.

CHAPTER 26

CULTURE AND CHRISTIANITY HAVE TO BE TRANSFORMED FOR THE GLORY OF GOD:

(Revelations 3:15-16) (KJV), one of the constant struggles of Christianity, both individually and corporately, is with culture. (PhilipYancy) Christians of today should take an example from the early Christians. They, without fear, had to stand firm in order for us to see the Christianity we are seeing today Some of the early Christians had to sacrifice their lives. What today's Christians have to bear in mind is that even Jesus did not find it easy, He became very unpopular. Christians had to discourage some of the cultures, which were practised by the Romans, such as men fighting with swords in the arena. Infanticide was very common yet it is killing of innocent lives. To them slavery was practiced, and was considered legal. Sexual trafficking was practised without any shame, yet Christianity said all the foregoing were an abomination unto the Lord. Therefore, Christians have to stand firm in order for the glory of God to reign. Culture is with us all the time so we have to be cautious with it so as not to be diluted with some cultural aspects, which are not Godly. Where should we stand, inside culture, outside, or ignore it, Christians should not try to isolate culture or segregate it. Christians should strive to go along with culture, to be able to transform it as we go along with life, as we ourselves should not go away from it, we should always strive to transform it. However, Christians are supposed to transform society faithfully. Christians get their role model from Jesus Christ who guaranteed Christians that he would be with them always even to the end of the world. Christians are called to transform culture because it has some aspects, which are not Godly. People should not be taken away from the world, as Jesus said in (John chapter 17:13-19) (KJV) asking the

Father not to take them away from the world, but keep them in the world to transform the world. Jesus had all authority from heaven and on earth. In (Matthew 28:18-20) (KJV) Jesus commissions Christians to go into the world, he did not mean them to go and be diluted by the world but for them to go and transform the world. That is the reason why he asked the Father to let them stay in the world, because he wanted them to stay for a purpose. It appears Christians are hesitant to take the world head on; on the other hand, it appears as if it was the world that was commissioned to go and make Christians dysfunctional.

At the same time he was commissioning them, he planted in their minds that when they go, they should bear in mind that they were the salt of the earth. The salt works like this, when it is in the food it mixes fully with the food that every part of the food will have salt, no more separation. Jesus likened us unto the salt, apart from transforming the taste of the food, salt is also self-preserving. Apart from transforming the world, Christians must have some qualities of self-discipline so they will not be diluted by the world.

CULTURE SOMETIMES DEVIATES FROM CHRISTIANITY:

Sometimes our cultural backgrounds may affect the way we understand scriptures. All humans who come to the Bible have some cultural backgrounds that mean we are struggling to separate these things so that we have a good understanding of each. Our habits, beliefs and practices sometimes can influence the whole community, nation or region. Normally the cultures shape our practices. Living in a community that rejects aspects of your culture, such as identity beliefs, or sexual orientation can have a negative impact on your wellbeing. The culture of God is the culture of love, so we need very to strive to understand the culture of God. If we look closely to that and all culture is like that we will have harmony in life. The faith may be referred to, as one true faith may be the religious concept that is believed to be superior to other beliefs. Culture is a way of life of groups of people, and the way they do things. Culture says there must be respect of human life that is Christianity also say, so that shows there is agreement of the two.

MORALITY IN CULTURE:

According to the Concise Oxford English Dictionary: moral means concerned with the principles of right or wrong behaviour, examining the nature of ethics and the foundations of good and bad character: morality in culture mean that we are looking at the good or the bad of the culture, which means we are looking at the cultural values, the codes of conduct or social mores (customs and conventions of a community) from a society that provides these codes of conduct in which it applies and is accepted by an individual. When we say morality in culture, we are looking at the customs and codes of conduct of that culture if they are acceptable to the individual or not. Therefore, when we are talking of morality in culture we are looking at the goodness or rightness of that culture. For culture to be accepted it has to show, distinguish, and be able to differentiate between proper and improper which are derived from a code of conduct from a particular philosophy, religion or culture. Moral development, focuses on the change and understanding of morality from infancy through adulthood, it develops through life to manhood and is influenced by the individual's experiences and their behaviour when faced with moral issues through different periods' physical and cognitive development. Morality concerns an individual's growing sense of what is right or wrong. When children are growing, they will be copying from adults the rights or the wrongs they do. Know that whatever you do someone is copying that.

CULTURE IN RELATIONSHIP WITH CHRISTIANITY:

The bubble of legalism cannot keep sin out of the church, and it hides one of God's most useful tools-us. ("The direct or indirect attachment of behaviours, disciplines, and practices to the belief in order to achieve salvation and right standing before God") emphasising a need "to perform certain deeds in order to gain. When we talk of legalism, it is when we base our justification on our own law-keeping rather than on the finished work of Christ. If we depend on our own merits, our own, efforts, even our own rituals, to make us acceptable before God, then we have become legalists. In short, legalism is salvation by works. We call this salvation-legalism.

It is this sort of legalism that Paul was fighting in the letter to the Galatians. Paul was clear that the Galatians had been deceived by the "The Judaizers" had taught another gospel altogether. "I am astonished that you are so quickly deserting him who called you in the grace of Christ are you turning to a different gospel" (Galatians 1) (KJV): Judaizers were teaching the people of Galatia that without being circumcised you cannot be acceptable in heaven. Paul was saying we have to have faith in Jesus. Let us avoid legalism in Christianity. Of course, the real gospel is; we are saved by grace alone, through faith alone in Christ alone- is such good news. In this gospel we are freed from the heavy yoke of works righteousness.

How was the early church affected by culture? The impact of Christianity on culture, the early church really brought to an end infanticide. To imagine that 2000 years later, the birth of Christ is still celebrated very fresh with the spirit that it is celebrated in. Think of all the heroes you may think of: they have come and gone, but this hero is celebrated anew. How powerful is that, even non-Christians will do it without thinking twice, bring any successful man in history and compare?

As culture and Christianity are living contemporarily, it is better to try and search where the problem might be hidden, it might be found that it is culture in the church that could be a problem. What happens is that sometimes the church would like to lure people from culture, but sometimes they will end up being diluted into culture, ending up being lukewarm Christians? There could be a problem in half-heartedness; becoming difficult for them to serve two masters, the church and culture, the church today is full of people who are half hearted otherwise we have to be fully transformed in order for us not to see a problem where there is no problem. Sometimes as Christians, we have to examine ourselves, because for anything to be good, it should start with you. How are we filled spiritually? We should always pray to be filled spiritually, as we have an example of Jesus speaking to the Samaritan woman, she was reminded that when worshiping, she had to bear in mind that she was worshiping a Spiritual God, hence she had to worship in truth and in Spirit. We have to transform ourselves into Spiritual beings as well in order to be in accord with the one we are worshiping. God is Spirit; whoever wants to be like Him must worship Him in truth and in Spirit.

According to Jesus here, we have to live a spiritual life ourselves. Let us examine our relationship with God, because He is Spirit, our approach must be spiritual. The woman of Samaria, when she was transformed, she would not ask Jesus if she could go and call others. The people who knew her before as the Samaritan woman, believed her at once because she was transformed, and they could see the transformation in her. We have to be transformed if we have to live an uncorrupted Christian life.

CULTURE WILL BE CORRUPTED IF IT IS OUTSIDE OF THE CHURCH:

Sometimes we Christians will corrupt the church because of the way we behave as Christians, yet Christians are to be exemplary. Let Christians be reminded that they are carrying Christianity on their shoulders as they go on with their daily lives. However, sometimes Christians are seen to compromise Christianity in order to accommodate culture. Since Christians claim to be followers of Christ, they must be seen to emulate Christ Himself who never bent to accommodate culture, knowing that if you would like to please culture you will end up being corrupted yourself. Christ came to earth to save us from the sin in which the devil had put us at time of Adam and Eve. It makes sense to say that if culture is outside of Christ, then it is without doubt that it is in that original sin. There is no conflict culture Christianity if culture is within the parameters of Christianity, because it will be known that it is corrected. What brings tension between culture and Christianity is a type of corrupted culture. For culture not to be tainted by corruption is for it stay closer to Christianity. Christians should always remember, "Christ is the transformer of culture". When we view the relationship that exists between these two, it must be viewed seriously basing on Christ who is of two natures, taking his divine nature seriously. (Culture Revisited) focusonthefamily.ca/content/Christ-and-culture) Culture was corrupted at the fall of man, but since Christ came to redeem us we are in the right direction if we are following Christ as He is above culture

When it comes to culture, it is not one size fit all, that means as cultures differ, we have to look at them closely and try to find what distance each culture is from Christ.

LAWS BASED AND THE GRACE OF GOD:

(John 1:14) (KJV) the main purpose of Jesus coming to earth and taking human nature, was to set an example. Let us look closely and note what he went through, and what he would do to overcome it. He is our model of eternal life, if we want to get eternal life. Law vs. Grace, there is so much conflict among Christians on the issue, one side says, "Salvation is by Grace and Grace alone". The other side counters that idea leads to lawlessness, God's standard in the law must be upheld. God's standard in the law must be, and Salvation is by Grace, but Grace alone comes to those who obey God's law. God's law is not there to condemn people, but to have a relationship between God and man. At the root of all this, we find differing opinions, the importance of the issue helps to fuel the intensity of the discussion:

When the Bible speaks of the law it refers to the detailed standard God gave to Moses, beginning in (Exodus 20) (KJV, with the Ten Commandments. The law will show a difference between those who keep the law and those who do not, there is holiness in those who keep the law because it means their relationship with God is close His law explains His requirements for a holy people, and include 3 categories: civil, ceremonial and moral laws. The law was given to separate God's people from the evil nations around them and to define sin, people who disobeyed and tried to mix with pagans were punished severely by being excluded from the temple of Jerusalem, which to them was an unbearable punishment (Ezra 10:11) (KJV). The biggest problem with us is that we do not examine ourselves thinking that we are perfect yet most of the time we sinning without noticing it, or even if we notice it we try to justify ourselves that we are fine. We must always confess our sins to do our part and grace does the rest, (Romans 5:13) (KJV), It is strange that sometimes we think that by keeping the laws without confessing, we are alright yet there are sins we did not notice, those do us harm. The law is there to remind us to examine revise and ourselves our relationship with God, which was once broken to pieces and was restored by Jesus, most of the actions we take are sinful without noticing them,(Romans 7:7) (KJV).

The law also clearly demonstrates that no human being could purify themselves enough to please God, that is, the law revealed our need for a Saviour.

By New Testament times, the religious leaders had made the law to suit themselves. They changed the law and added to it their own rules and traditions, (7:7-9) (KJV) while the law its self was good: it was weak in that it lacked the power to change a sinful heart. (Romans 8:3) (KJV), keeping the law as interpreted by the Pharisees, had become oppressive and overwhelming burden. (Luke 11:46) (KJV). It was this legalistic climate that Jesus came, and conflict with the Pharisees because they pretended to have high standards and noble beliefs which they did not have. However, Jesus the law giver, said, "Do not think that I have come to abolish the laws or the Prophets; I have not come to abolish them, but to fulfil them". (Matthew 5:17) (KJV) the law was not evil, it served as a mirror to reveal the condition of a person's heart,(John 1:17) (KJV) says, "For the law was given through Moses, Grace and truth came through Jesus Christ" Jesus embodied the perfect Balance between Grace and law, (John 1:14) (KJV).

God has always been full of Grace(Psalms 116:5; (KJV) (Joel 2:13) (KJV) and people have always been saved by faith in God (Genesis 15:6) (KJV).

CHAPTER 27

JESUS' MISSION ON EARTH WAS TO GIVE US A DIVINE REVELATION:

Jesus' main purpose of coming to earth was to establish the peace heavenly peace provided by God. This is the main centre of Jesus' preaching. We need to be filled by the divine heavenly Spirit. This is when Jesus began to act as king of peace. God manifested Himself on earth. (Matthew 3:2) (KJV), the peace from heaven started to establish on earth when John the Baptist started preaching in the wilderness. He was saying repent for the kingdom of heaven is at hand. To repent is to turn from all those deeds that are ungodly. The things that are ungodly are: lying, cheating, stealing gossiping, revenge, abuse and sexual immorality. Turning completely from these things is to repent, once you are free from these, the kingdom of heaven has been established in you. So when we are saying, thy kingdom come, we are saying Lord clean my heart so that I am free from all these things, if you are free from all these things, then the kingdom is established in you. Let your good works be seen on earth, and then the kingdom has already come.

Without the real revelation, people might be involved in some unexplained supernatural powers or events. (Ephesians 6:12) (KJV). (Reknew. og/2015/01/05-this reminds us to be on our guard against the powers of darkness which come unnoticed, these are the forces of darkness which are fighting against Christianity, Christians are warned not to sit back and expect things to be plain sailing. We must keep on asking Christ to give us His Holy Spirit which will enable us to be able to fight against this and win. Jesus came to set an example of the kingdom of heaven on earth, and to show us the way to Calvary where we can get God's eternal, life. The people of the kingdom of heaven graciously embrace others and sacrificing themselves in serving others. It consists of people trusting and employing "power under" rather than "power over" even when they, like Jesus suffer because this. That will be imitating their saviour who died for them and for all the people. It consists on people submitting to God's rule and doing His will, this resembles God's kingdom. Jesus' kingdom is not of this world, because it contrasts the kingdom of this world in every possible way.

THE WORLDLY DOMINION DIFFERENT FROM THE HEAVENLY REALM:

The earthly dominion contrasts the way of doing things to the heavenly realm. They differ in five things:

1. The dominion of the world trusts the power of the sword, Jesus who came to set an example, did not trust the power of the sword, we have to be emulating Him, and Jesus carried His own cross to Calvary, meaning that the realm of God trusts the power of the cross. It contrasts with the dominion of this world in every possible way. Their way of doing, things are very different from each other. The people of the realm of God love one another, their service is for one another, as it is, and we have to choose which power we are to take the sword or the cross. (Philippians 3:10) (KJV) the reason why I would recommend the power of the cross is that because from that cross we see the power of resurrection which is a sure promise for us that we may as well resurrect if we follow Him. (Romans 1:16) (KJV) we should not be ashamed of the cross for we know that the way of the cross leads to salvation, which is what every Christian is looking for, salvation in the end.

2. The dominion of the world controls behaviour. If they do not comply; it will use force, the reason is simple, at the fall of man, and man lost control of the dominion he was given. If we fallow Jesus' example, that will mean we will be with Him in glory when He comes in His glory. The kingdom of heaven transforms lives from inside out. The kingdom of the world is rooted in advancing

one's self-interests and one's own will, while the realm of heaven is centred on carrying out God's will, even if this requires sacrificing one's own interests.

3. The dominion of the world is tribal in nature, it is for us to ask God to transform us so that we conform to the heavenly realm, that can only happen through His grace and mercy, the earthly dominion is heavily interested in defending, and advancing the interests of one's own people. Group or one's ethnicity, one's state, one's ideologies one's religion, or one's political agenda. That is why it is a rule characterised by perpetual conflicts. The ruling of heaven is however universal, for it is centred on simply loving as God loves. It is centred on people living for the sole purpose of (replicating) i.e. making one the exact copy of Jesus, copying the love of Jesus Christ to all people at all times in all places without condition.

4. The rule of the world is a tit-for-tat kind of settling scores; its motto is eye for an eye, and tooth for a tooth. In this fallen world no one wants the type of settling things the way Jesus did; it is not in them the world cannot survive on loving its enemies and blessing those who persecute you; it carries the sword not the cross. Jesus is not really concerned with solving the political problems of this world, but rather He is concerned with our salvation. Sometimes the rule of this world comes disguised as the heavenly one, how do we know that it is a worldly rule? Jesus came to establish the heavenly realm, even without saying a word Jesus gave us a very good example of Himself, if we could follow exactly how He lived His life, and we will not go wrong. They insisted on making Him a political leader, but He did not take it up, all He did was to ensure that the people get the salvation, which was His mission here on earth that is the biggest thing people failed to understand that He was a soul saviour and not a political liberator. Instead of being a politician, Jesus requires us to care for the need, because that is what He Himself cared for them most and He will always be with you if you do care for the need, He even said at one time that the need you will always have them. If we could follow His footsteps, we can be guaranteed eternal life.

Let us not forget that eternal life is our main goal, if we are like that we will be in coordination with Him because that is what He came here for. This must be written in the book of our hearts that the participants of the heavenly realm of God carry the cross not the sword, they are not to return evil with an evil, violence with violence. We are to manifest the unique salvation of Christ by returning evil with good, turning other cheek, going the second mile, loving, praying for our enemies. Far from seeking retaliation, we seek the well-being of our enemies.

5. The dominion of the world has earthly enemies. It is always fighting earthly battles, this should be a good reminder to us for we have seen wars being fought in the name of seeking peace on earth, but peace is never there. Infect it keeps on getting worse, which should be a good lesson to us that we should be taking and carrying our cross by now. We always aim to emulate what Jesus gave us as an example. When He was giving this example it was not easy, see how He carried His cross to Calvary, it appears we are looking for the easy ones, which will not take us near to Him, yet we must strive to be participants of the realm of heaven, which we now know its requirements. Let us ask to be provided with the generous providence. This will make us see what is done in heaven, but not only see it but put it into our life application. This will be in accordance with the provision of God who has no earthly enemies. The disciples of the kingdom of heaven are committed to loving their enemies. (Philippians 3:20) (KJV) reminds us that if we comply with what Jesus requires us to do we will be automatically the citizens of this kingdom.The citizens of this kingdom do the will of the Father of heaven and they treat everyone there as friends and neighbours. There is a warfare that the kingdom of God is involved in; it is not against the enemies of blood and flesh. It is rather against the rulers, against the authorities, against the cosmic power of this present darkness; against spiritual forces of evil forces in the heavenly places.

THE RELIGIOUS LEADERS IN THE GOSPELS:

Jesus was faced with a task of trying to explain to the religious leaders who always accused him of trying to do away with their culture. Yet Jesus had come to fulfil the laws and make their culture Godly, Jesus was always at loggerheads with the Pharisees because they regarded themselves as superior to others, so they wanted to keep themselves separate ones, they regarded themselves superior to tax collectors, gentiles, and other sinners. They regarded their beliefs as foundational which means they regarded themselves as superior, they were regarded as separatists, were known for their self-righteousness and they had a religious pride. The word Pharisee means, "separated" which has been handed down to our generation as our current life application indicates. Some people amongst us want to be separated, thinking of themselves as separated from others. They were outnumbered in the Sanhedrin by the Sadducees, but they were influential because they had majority support in the community. Most of them were leaders in the synagogues and had control of them, making some changes in the law to suit them and wanted others to obey them which they themselves did not obey. That is the reason why they were in conflict with Jesus. They accepted that the written word was inspired by God which means there we agree with them. (Matthew 9:14) (KJV); Sometimes Jesus disagreed with them they had a strict rule on fasting, yet Jesus said let the people do it. (Luke 11:42) (KJV); to follow Jesus must be to sympathise with the need, not being selfish. (Mark 7:7) (KJV), instead of teaching the truth about Jesus sometimes they teach the doctrines which are anti-Christ sometimes we worship God for the wrong motive. Jesus Himself identified Himself with the sinners, He associated with the poor, and we are also expected to do the same. We are to always do the will of God in order for us to inherit the kingdom of heaven. Jesus did not like their hypocrisy way of behaving, He says worship must be motivated by love not to be seen by men.

JESUS REALLY DID NOT WANT TO DO AWAY WITH RELIGION AND CULTURE:

(BBC 1 August 2019) It has been historically proved that those who follow Christ have never gone wrong. For two thousand years, Christianity has survived the test of times. The writer of this article is arguing that "it is the nature of religions to come and go", giving an example of some religions that have come and gone, giving examples of religions such as Zoroaster, which was a dominant religion but it is now no more. The writer is likening Christianity to that, saying that in its early stages, Christianity was intact, but now it fragmented into opposing factions. The writer gives as an example, "the early apostles were prepared to martyrs defending Christianity, but it is no more the case today". (Psychologytoday.com of 15 January 2017), also seem to agree with BBC, BBC of 23 May 2019 is saying, "Iraq has shown a big decline in its Christian population, Christians are failing to defend their religion, it is giving in." (focusonthefamily.com of 1 January 2014) gives encouraging ideas, saying "let us get an example from Paul the apostle, it was not easy at all but he persevered. Jesus Christ Himself did not say it was going to be easy for us, He warned us that we would find it difficult, if it was difficult for Him, how easy is it going to be for us?" It is better for Christians to rely on the scriptures because they are inspired by God to help us to stand against trying times and come out of them stronger than ever before. What is required is to surrender ourselves to Him and He will use us according to the way He would like us to be, not us dictate to Him what to do. Let us ask for His divine guidance, so that we do not do it our way of thinking. Let us look at the Bible how it is, things in it are inter woven in such a way that they are meant to lead us to salvation. When we use our intelligence they should be guided by divine guidance, so that in the end we are part of the trinity. If we are guided by Him we will never be out of step or out of the realities of life.

(*Thompson Mandaza 07.03.2018*) The Israelites in Exodus, Leviticus and Deuteronomy got various punishments because they defied God and embarked on their unholy behaviours.

CHRISTIAN REVELATION IS PRESERVED IN THE BIBLE FOR HIS LOVED ONES:

(The Trumpet.com) accessed 27 May 2020: God inspired the Bible to be written in order for Him to be revealed to His people. It was not all written at one time, but in phases. The Book of Revelations says it all; it shows how the Lord wants to be friendly to man. All God wants us to hear or to do is revealed in the scripture. With the fact that God inspires it, it has survived the test of times than any other book that has ever been written. (2 Timothy 3:16-17) (KJV) says all scripture is inspired by God.

THE PERSECUTION OF BELIEVERS WORLDWIDE:

The way believers are being persecuted has taken a new turn. The devil is now very tactful, and is now using psychological persecution. The devil has also found way in multiculturalism. The authorities will not let you do Christian works; they say you will offend others, because we are now a multicultural nation. There is no way we could run away from this persecution of believers, for the Lord Himself went through such, for He was also persecuted. As we follow His footsteps, we are also going through such suffering as well. Some religions are more persecuted than other religions (2 Timothy 3:12) (KJV) gives us the examples of other believers who also underwent persecution because of their belief in Christ Jesus, we should not think that this has happened to us alone. (https://www. bbc.co.uk) accessed 13 June 2020. Politics has a hand in the persecution of believers. Where the believers are pleading with politicians for human rights, they are taken like they want to their power away. They are only saying that the people belong to God hence, they have to be treated as equals to the politicians. That now needs some revelation that it is only a deep concern for the good life of their fellow people, and not to take over their powers. Although some countries have now got hidden persecution there are some this present day as mentioned by the BBC, as reported on 3 May 2019, countries like Sri-Lanka, and China have been mentioned as still burning churches and killing Christians. The number of those suffering in these countries is as high as one person in every three people, which shows how Christians are suffering worldwide. These countries are fighting to wipe Christianity from their countries or from the face of the earth. In countries like Iraq only 1.5 million are Christians and Palestine Christians have gone down to be as little as 1.5%because many people are running away from those countries, fearing for their lives. It appears that although some countries are not persecuting Christian, but they are taking this lightly, with organisations such as the United Nations (UN) not taking human life seriously. Therefore, we can see how these countries have planted fear in all the people who would like to be Christians. Christians are pleaded with to take those persecuted as them, because as Christians we were commissioned by Jesus to take His word all-over the world so that everyone has the world.

THE EARLY BELIEVERS SUFFERED PERSECUTION BECAUSE IT WAS GOD'S PLAN TO SPREAD HIS WORD:

(1 Peter 4:16) (KJV) "If you suffer as a Christian, do not be ashamed, but praise God that you bear that name" why were Christians persecuted? How was it that they underwent such? If Christians see these things happening to them they will know that they are following in the footsteps of Jesus for He Himself went through such. These things are still happening today, but they could be happening in a slightly different way, we have to be watchful and see how we can handle them in the name of the Lord. All what we are seeing today is not new, it happened to those who were before us, it is still happening. (luke 6:22-23) (KJV) when these things are happening to Christians, they must weigh them and value them according to the earthly kingdom and heavenly kingdom, it is up to Christians to value the two kingdoms. As Jesus was sending us into the world He did not promise us comfort, what He only promised us was that "I will be with you all way". Those are very comforting words, we have to endure the persecution until the end. As the Saviour suffered for our sake, so was the early church in the first two centuries. Jesus always prayed to the Father "As I am in your Father, and we are one, I would like them to be in me" Since the early Christians were following Jesus, they had to be like him in both Spirit and in deeds. This means that we have to take it up from where they left off until we hand it over to the next generation, with the help of Him who suffered for our sake.

PLAQUES FOR GODS AND GODDESSES:

Christians in those days suffered a lot because so many people resisted the change from Judaism to Christianity. The other factor that made them suffer was that pagans surrounded them. Some of whom made money by making plaques for their gods or goddesses. When people were following Christ, they could not buy those plaques; the makers of those plaques were going out of business, which was another reason for Christians to be hated. Another reason was that Christians could not participate in some pagan rituals. These factors created a big tension between culture and Christianity, which prompted the writer to have desire to research and gather information from both sides. As the research is carried out, it is becoming clear whether those who said they were being put out of business and that their culture was being killed were right or not. Alternatively, those who said Christianity was the representative of the heavenly kingdom on earth and not there to kill culture. During the Roman Empire, (which lasted for twelve centuries) people worshipped different gods and goddesses in whom they put all their faith. They were worshipped in temples, animals were slaughtered as they thought that the blood of animals was the best sacrifices, and this was the way they communicated with their gods. Even to this day, some still believe that the blood of animals can purify them hence animals are still slathered to that effect.

THE PERSECUTION OF THE EARLY BELIEVERS HELPED THE CHURCH TO GROW:

(Acts 8:1-40) (KJV): God works in a mysterious way, when the early believers were persecuted, they were scattered all over Judea and Samaria yet it was God's way of spreading the gospel. Sometimes in life when you forced out of your comfort zone you are sometimes forced to change the way you do things. In (Acts 1:8) (KJV) Jesus promised His disciples that they would receive power, when power is from the Holy Spirit, it will turn everything to work for the good of the Lord. From those days God has not changed, it is us who do change, otherwise even today when we face hardships, they meant to further the work of God, when we face hardships in life let us turn that into the good of the Lord. The advice is that when we face hardships let us communicate with Him what He means to us with that hardship, most of the time it is meant for furtherance of His works on earth. Let us from this learn to ask the Lord when we in hardships to ask the what H e wants us to do genuinely and honestly, He will tell us what to do and He will guide us, because if He did it then, why not now. Sometime the environment in which we live may pull us back, yet this is the reason for these examples for us to be able to turn all that seem to be bad times for the good of the Lord

CULTURE HAS TO BE TRANSFORMED FOR THE GLORY OF GOD:

(desiringgod.org) accessed 24.08.2020. Since culture is known as our way of living, Christians are urged to live a life, which is exemplary so the glory of the Lord may be seen in us. Culture itself is not bad, but only that it is sometime corrupted, so it is up to us Christians to try to do good so as to correct some of the corruption in culture, model culture through your own behaviour. We should see the elements that are not perfect, and try to perfect them, those elements of culture that good, let us encourage them for the good of Christianity. We do wrong to God most of the time, but He forgives us, we should not take that as a weakness. We should come to Him thanking Him and giving all the glory to Him. Culture is with us all the time meaning that it is in our habits, our language, our customs, and all things that we cannot live without. We have to be careful what we do so as not go astray. Culture means our beliefs and values, so in this case we have to be careful what we value in life. Is it not conflicting with the will of God, so our behaviour has to be in the confines of the Lord in order for us not to go astray?

WHEN A SOCIETY IS ZEALOUS FOR CULTURAL DIVERSITY IT WILL STRUGGLE TO ACCOMMODATE CHRISTIANITY:

If anything, Christianity could not be surprised with cultural diversity, because in Christianity was started not of a single culture but a diversity of cultures. All religions have their accepted principles of rules that cannot be questioned (dogma), or articles of belief, those followers must accept without question. This can lead to inflexibility and intolerance in the face of other beliefs. (It is essential that we take into account everyone's needs in the design and the delivery of services). Religious extremists can contribute to conflict escalation. (When we try to fill God's purpose, we must make sure that it does not inconvenience others). They see radical measures as necessary to fulfilling God's wishes. (God's wishes cannot be fulfilled by forcing others).

Globalisation brings a culture of pluralism, meaning religions "with overlapping but distinctive ethics and interests" interact with one another. As a result, globalisation brings to the light the fact that since religions has similar values, not one of them is "correct" and therefore can be changed.

A range of factors such as where the person lives, their gender and their language can influence cultural needs. They can include how soon a person would like their funeral, whether they like to be buried or cremated, and any rituals or ceremonies that are important to them. Globalisation refers to the historical process by which all worlds' people increasingly come to live in a single social unit. It implicates religion and religions in several ways. From religious of perspectives, globalisation calls fourth religious response and interpretation.

The major consequences of globalisation have been transmogrification of traditional religions and belief systems; the beginning of disintegration of traditional social fabrics and shared norms by consumerism, cyber-culture, new-fangled religions and changing work ethics and work rhythms; the fast spreading.

Globalisation has therefore had the paradoxical effect of making religions (via their religious leaders and clites) more self-conscious of themselves as being world religions though religion is strengthened and fortified by globalisation it represents a challenge to its (globalisation)hybridizing effects. Depending on where you live, religion may make you also feel better about yourself by making you feel part of your larger culture. People who are religious have higher self- esteem and better psychological adjustment than people who aren't, according to a January 2012 study.

CHAPTER 28

SALVATION HISTORY OF MAN:

"For God so loved the world that He gave His only begotten Son that who so ever believes in Him should not perish but have everlasting life (KJV)". So many thousands of years before the Messiah could come. God loved humankind from the very beginning when He said, let us make man in our image. In the image of God does not mean in the physical image, but resembling God spiritually, and was given dominion over everything. Salvation history is the way we had gone astray into the captivity of Satan. Jesus ransomed and redeemed us, so who are we in this world, what are we meant to be? The story of salvation starts with the creation of Adam and Eve and how the fall of man came about through the lies of the devil. Before the fall, when God created man, He wanted him to join the Trinity, before man chose to go his own way. Salvation history is very interesting in that is both past present and future, because the story of salvation is not over yet. God plans well in advance, He planned the coming of the Messiah at creation. (Acts 4:12) (KJV) for there is no salvation in any other: C(ol. 1:15-17) (KJV) Jesus is the image of God, he invites us to be like him so that we can be in the image of God. (Rev. 1:8 Rev. 21:6) (KJV) when we talk about Christ we have to bear in mind he is the past, present and future. We are tasked to take this wonderful story to the next generation. The religions of Islam, Judaism and Christianity are monotheistic religions. Only Christianity is the religion of a person Jesus Christ the God-Man. Salvation history means the story of God and man, God loved and cherished mankind, but man walked away from God, he walked away from Godly riches to rags, and back again. However, Jesus

Christ is the rescuer, he came down from his throne to share his life and deliver humankind from captivity. Quite literally, the story of salvation history is the story of how we are saved, our redemption in Jesus Christ, but it is actually much more, we have to understand how we are in the world and what we are meant to be.

The reason why the Bible goes hand in hand with culture is that, culture is our day-to-day association and our everyday existence, as the Bible is, when we were delivered on earth, we were delivered with an instruction manual. That is the reason why Culture and the Bible go hand in glove; the problem arises when we try to separate them. When we talk of the Bible as an instruction manual, there is a temptation of likening it to the commercial instruction manual. This instruction manual was inspired by Him and made Holy. For us to be able to understand it, we must always seek His divine revelation and guidance when consulting this manual. As man had gone his own way, consulting this manual means we are trying to find our way back, ultimately seeking to participate in His salvation plan. There is a place of hope and change where man can find happiness.

The "postmodern strategic plan" is failing, and leading to chaos and despair: family breakdowns, family revolting against family, nation is rising against nation, war after war, with never ending of wars in sight. All these wars are fought in the name of seeking peace on earth which is never there. Blood is spilt every day in the name of seeking peace on earth, and it goes without noticing that instead of achieving it, we are creating the opposite. There is always gender and race conflict with no end in sight, antagonism between economic and social classes and warfare between ideologies and nations.

THE RELATIONSHIP THAT IS THERE BETWEEN GOD AND MAN STARTED AT CREATION:

Science teaches us that Jesus is in His Father, He prays to the Lord to that Father I pray that these stay here on earth and represent the heavenly kingdom here on earth, incarnation is when the Lord becomes a person, if that is the case, and it means we are like Him. Christians believe that

Jesus in the Son of God. Man was made in the image of God, so we automatically qualify to be in the trinity that is the truth that is there and is the undisputed truth. If one of the trinity resurrected from the dead, that means we are assured of the resurrection.

How does man resemble God?

THE DOMINION THAT WAS GIVEN MAN BY GOD:

As God created man in His image, He gave him dominion to rule over everything on earth. However, at the fall of man, he lost that dominion, but now man is struggling to regain that lost dominion. Man is trying to do it in such a way that it will still honour God. Dominion really means to rule over when we oppress or misuse, we have gone out of step we need to come back to terms and abide by the terms of the dominion. To have dominion means to be in charge of the world on behalf of God. A man must strive to give life to everything on earth, not to be killing for the sake of killing like a leopard, which kills for the sake of killing. Dominion, finding and fulfilling your purpose in life. With His word, God spoke to humankind. He gave instruct ructions on what we are here to do. To be fruitful, means to of use to God. To replenish the earth, means the earth to look good because we are there. The man was given a mandate, command or authorisation to act in a particular way on public issues. The right of a man to rule is derived from divine authority.

HOW THE KINGDOM OF GOD SHOULD BE RECEIVED ON EARTH:

The kingdom of God should be composed of n people who should not be greedy, because greediness will lead to corruption. People of the kingdom should always feel for others not being selfish. When you do something good, you should feel to want to do better than that in future. Even when you have a position of authority, you must not make life difficult for those under your authority. When you do all those good things it will mean you are making the kingdom to come on earth. The kingdom of heaven in

Christianity means the spiritual realm over which God reigns as king, or the fulfilment on earth of God's will. Jesus mostly used this word primarily in the gospels. Luke 17; 21 The Pharisees asked Jesus when the kingdom of God would come, not knowing that the kingdom had already come. The kingdom of God is not like an earthly kingdom with geographical boundaries. It begins with the work of God's Spirit in people's lives and relationships. We must stop looking on programmes with evidence of God's kingdom. We should look for what God is doing in people's hearts.

What is human nature?
How can man join the Trinity?
What should a man do to earn Salvation?
What was God's redemption plan?
What is the work of the Holy Spirit?

The Holy Spirit who was said by Jesus is the comforter, one who will plead with God on our behalf "intercedes", or supports, or acts as an advocate, particularly in times of trial. The Holy Spirit acts not only to plead with God, but will also plead with the sinner for the sinner to repent their sin so as to be able to be accepted into the fold. They are accepted back into the fold because the Holy Spirit has convinced the unredeemed person both of the fullness of their action and their moral as sinners before God. The gifts of the Holy Spirit are to give us wisdom and to give us understanding, to counsel to give us fortitude, to give us knowledge of the piety and fear of the Lord. While some Christians accept this as definitive list of specific attributes, others understand them merely as examples of the Holy Spirit's work through the faithful. The Holy Spirit is essential in our lives for spreading the word of God. The disciples were told not to do anything until they were filled clothed with the Holy Spirit. When the Holy Spirit came at Pentecost, the disciples started to do God's work without any fear "We must ask in prayer for this Holy Spirit for He will change our lives". The presence of the Holy Spirit is a requirement to serve God in this life. The Holy Spirit controls the believer who yields to God and submits himself to God's work. When these conditions are met, the believer lives in the power of the Spirit and produces the fruit of the spirit. The Holy Spirit indwells the believer permanently.

What guides the Church and it's People?
Is the Church sustained by the Holy Spirit?
How does Christianity establish Relationship with God?
How can Christians live in peace with God?

Scholars have been debating this issue for years. It is a matter of debate for scholars; some say we are justified by works, some say we are justified by faith. The school of thought says, we will be doing the works if we have faith. If we have faith, we have peace with God through our Lord Jesus Christ. We have peace of God, even God's peace in us though both those things are also true. Let us give God His place; He is the one who can justify us. We cannot justify ourselves, no matter how much we might think we are doing well. If we have faith, He can have mercy on us, and in addition, He can justify us. Stop waring and you can be at peace. Jesus did not promise us peace because even He Himself was accused. However, He promises us peace at the end. Wars are being fought today saying that we want peace. Yet peace is never there. To love God is to love Him with all your heart, with all our strength and with all our possession Have peace in your heart and be obedient to God all your life. Christians should always try to be peaceful, that will be following in Jesus' footsteps. We are created to worship God, The laws of God are not harsh, but they are to give us good relationship with Him. The politicians promise you peace but it is peace by silencing you, it is peace by silencing you with a sword that he carries. Let us ask for the peace to start with us. You cannot have it physically, because the world is rocky. Galatians says the fruit of the spirit is peace. Let us ask for the fruit of peace in our hearts. Are we going to achieve peace with nuclear weapons? Let peace begin with you value human life, every human is created in the image of God.

THE CHURCH CANNOT EMBRACE CULTURE WITHOUT EMBRACING IDOLS:

If the church is going to take culture as whole, then we will have some problems, because that would mean that they will bring idols in the church. The church today is faced with a challenge because it appears the church is in the decline, so when the church wants to lure people back into the church, it appears it may want to relax some of the rules. This would mean urging people to come as they are, then culture will start thinking that they are allowed to come with their idols. The multi-culturalisms is where culture and Christianity will be conflicting, Christianity is facing resistance from many angles. It is facing resistance from politicians, culture and from multi-culturalism, on the other hand, those who are in the church did not come whole-heartedly, but only for saying, my religion is Christianity without being convicted spiritually. The problem faced with Christians today is of double standards, because a Christian fears that if I say no to sin then I become very unpopular. What does it help a Christian to gain popularity without following what Jesus taught, He taught us very well that what is it to gain the world and lose your soul? As Christians, pray every day they are asking the Lord to give them courage to be able to fight the forces of darkness. Sometimes we are of a mentality that what people are going to say, without taking into account that we are not fighting the people but sin, which we know very well that it represents the forces of darkness. The problem is now that we are afraid of what will people say, without asking, but what will God say, it appears we are not winning at all, when Jesus says those who worship Him must worship Him in spirit and in truth. Where are we now?

CHAPTER 29

JESUS CHRIST THE DIVINE STRATEGIST:

Since the beginning, God's plan is to allow man to share in His blessed life. Satan rejected God's plan, he was irreversibly cast out from heaven and has sought to corrupt man ever since. Adam failed to follow God's clear direction, (Genesis 1:28 (KJV) to protect the garden. (Genesis 2:15) (KJV) tells us that Adam and Eve were put in the Garden of Eden to look after it properly and were given instructions which defined what they could do and what they could not do (Genesis 2:17) (KJV). Adam and Eve had a choice to obey or disobey, but they chose to disobey, the reader is reminded that we still have that choice, but let us pray to be enabled to obey.

Adam and Eve were cast out of Eden into the world to be tormented by sin and death.(Genesis 3:15-24) (KJV) rather than enjoying the paradise of Eden planned by God, man struggles in the chaotic battle between God and evil.

Jesus Christ the eternal king and divine strategist come to proclaim the plan of the Gospel. Jesus had a strategy from the beginning; He is with the Father from the beginning, (John 1:1-5) (KJV). Rather than a long string of events, John's story has its beginning and end in God's blessing. Creation is the foundation of all the love of God and His saving plans. Read (John 17:21-23) B (KJV), Jesus very much liked his disciples to become one. We must help so that the people become one. Mad in one accord. Jesus prayed for us to have unity among ourselves first, then unite with Him and the Father there must be good relationship among us all. God's strategy of salvation is to send His Son into the world, (John 3:16) (KJV) For God to give us the Bible which

He helps to re veal is his plan of salvation to man. The devil comes when we are unaware, and takes our minds away from that goodness. What the Lord is trying to build in us, the devil tries to spoil by his lies. The devil wants to separate us from God so his plan to save man from sin, will fail. (Matthew 1:21) (KJV). The plan for Jesus to come into the world was to save man from the original sin. It is not enough to say that Jesus died on the cross to save us from sins without us asking Him to take control of our lives. The coming of Jesus fulfils the Old Testament prophesies.

At Emmaus Jesus explains the meaning of the Old Testament to the disciples, filling them with owe, (Luke 24:32) (KJV). The incarnation reveals that the hidden meaning of the Old Testament is the dying of the Saviour for our sins, (1 Cor. 15:3-5) (KJV) there will always be people who doubt the resurrection, yet so many people witnessed it, that was the reason why He stayed forty days after the resurrection and before the ascension.

CULTURE AND THE SALVATION OF MAN:

Jesus' coming as a Messiah was foretold in the creation at the beginning of time. God is known from the beginning as three in one, and He is still known as the trinity. Trinity: Father, Son and Holy Spirit. The Lord's qualities are known as; Truth, Love and Fullness of mercy. He created and sustains everything that He created His divine revelation is in the Holy Spirit, which guides the church and His people. For sending His Son into the earth as a sacrifice was His redemption plan. God is the author of Scriptures through His inspiration, and He divinely reveals it to His people. Searching Scriptures reveals His Holiness to us, sacred Christ sacred scriptures and sacred tradition, magisterium (some teaching exercised by bishops) authority to interpret the Bible, His whole plan being to open man's mind to know His kingdom. Man did not do anything that deserves salvation, but it is only by the grace of God.

HOW MULTI- CULTURALISM BECAME A CONTROVERSIAL ISSUE, AND HOW IT BECAME A CAUSE OF DISAGREEMENT:

CHAPTER 30

CHRISTIANITY:

Christianity is a religion based upon the teachings and miracles of Jesus, Jesus is the Christ, and Christ means the anointed one. Refer to (John 1:1) (KJV) "In the beginning was the Word, and the Word was with God, and the Word was God. (Verse 14) (KJV), and the Word was made flesh, and dwelt among us,(and we beheld His glory, the glory as of the only begotten of the Father,) full of grace and truth." Jesus is both God and man. "All who welcome Jesus Christ as Lord of their lives are reborn spiritually, receiving new life from God. Through faith in Christ, this new birth changes us from the inside out-rearranging our attitudes, desires and motives. Being born makes you physically alive, and places you in your parents' family. Being reborn makes you spiritually alive and puts you in God's family (John1:12) (KJV) ". Have you asked Christ to make you a new person? Christ is not Jesus' second name. He fulfilled the Old Testament prophesies which said there would come a Messiah.

Jesus has two natures, divine as well as human, and is worth of praise and prayer. Christianity teaches that there is only one God in all existence, He made the universe, the earth and created Adam and Eve, He created man in His own image. This does not mean that God has a body of flesh and bones. Image means the likeness of God's character and rationality (the goodness of it). As we were made in the image of God, every person is worth of respect and honour.

This means that we did not evolve through a random process from a single celled organism, into rational immortal beings. Christianity teaches that God is a trinity: Father, Son and Holy Spirit. Christianity means establishing relationship with God, living in peace with God and with each other.

Christianity keeps culture in check; otherwise, if it were not kept in check, culture would end up making idols for worship. Now the question arises: Is the church going to embrace culture without embracing idols? Is it not that culture was perfect, but corrupted by human sin? Christ himself is God and is sovereign, instead of trying to compare him with beings.

Instead of it being openly, there is a polite persecution of believers worldwide. If cultural expression is outside the church, it may be corrupted by sin, if they are existing contemporarily, which one will be compromised to accommodate the other? Cultural expressions are good, but they have to be augmented and perfected by Christian revelation and the work of the church, because Christ is supreme to everything.

It would be said, culture is a good expression tainted by sin, and hence the need for Christ to cleans it. If it is tainted by sin that would mean that, there is tension between culture and Christianity, which needs cleansing. That would mean looking at culture closely and see what aspects of culture should be left out.

What is the relationship between culture and Christianity?

CHRISTIANITY HAS TO PERFECT SOME ELEMENTS OF CULTURE THAT ARE NOT GODLY:

It has to be taken into account that human beings are representing God here on earth. Therefore, it is better to always practise some Holiness as we live in our day-to-day activities. When we strive to always, do good, means we are practising what is always done in heaven. Everything is Holy in heaven that means we will be practising Holiness while we are still here on earth. When we always pray that thy kingdom come, and thy will be done on earth as it is in heaven, We should try to do good like what is done in heaven by doing so we are bringing the heavenly kingdom on earth by our deeds. We must try to achieve that by keeping Holy standards, if we try to keep away from sin we are upholding God's standards. If those around us see our good works, they will emulate them. Christ himself came to set an example of how life should be always. All his ways are shown in the bible, all what God wants and what he does not want is all outlined in the Bible. Jesus showed us the way to be always in touch with Him through prayer as Jesus himself always done, because our relationship with God is maintained through prayer. Our eyes must always be focused on God devotedly. (Romans 13:13) (KJV) because we belong to Him, we must live decent lives for all to see and follow.

We have to keep on evaluating our lives to see if we have not moved away from the original. Our lives must always be kept in check. (Exodus chapters 31-39) (KJV) give us guide lines, because it is easy to be carried away into culture alone, without being kept in check Biblically. "Culture and the Bible" How do you react when you are surrounded by family and friends who do not believe in Christ?

CULTURE IS NOT BY INSTRUCTION BUT BY OSMOSIS:

CHRIST ABOVE CULTURE:

Sometimes the message of Christ is a threat to the power and influence of cultural directions. It disapproves or criticises some of what culture does, that is, dishonest and fraudulent conduct in culture wanting to gain control over others and keep them subjected as slaves. It points out where we are made to believe that something is right when it is wrong, a faulty judgement. Putting an effort to achieve, to control in a skilful way and damages the purity of each other. That is the reason we are asked to stay in prayer to avoid temptations because sin does not care who you are, even the Son of God was tempted. At times, the most Christian thing to do is to do our things typically with the aim of persuading others to share our view. In addition, showing an accurate and deep understanding of a detailed analysis and assessment of something philosophically that reveals the unwelcome results of sin. This takes a systematic investigation into something, in order to establish facts and reach new conclusions. To be able to show how Aeschylus 'view of how to pull or twist out of shape the people living together in a more orderly community. Or to set out the ideas or features which are opposed to one another in a Marxist reading of Augustine does a service to readers. It teaches us a truer way. Of course, such a position has its dangers for us. Unlike Christ, we can easily be led stray by fallen angels ourselves. Sometimes there is creative and systematic work undertaken to increase the stock of knowledge. This is done by collecting, organising, and analysing of information to increase understanding of a topic or issue. Sometimes it is to show us why something is wrong and sometimes puts us at risk of ending up displaying an overly critical point of view. This gives a characteristic of false pride; having an exaggerated sense of self-importance, not prepared to learn from another and mistaking our own voice for that of Christ's. To help us, then, Christians need more than one stance in regards to culture.

CHRISTIANITY AND CULTURE ARE PARADOX:

Christianity and culture seem to contradict each other, but a close look reveals that, there are minute differences, which need clarification. The difference between culture and Christianity requires divine revelation. We must be able to categorise these differences, because of the smallness of the differences, it has caused many to live double standards.(2 Timothy 3:16) (KJV), although Scriptures seem to be rebuking culture, it appears as it is rebuking yet it is the way it corrects and smoothens when there are some aspects of culture which are not perfect. Culture and Christianity seem to be conflicting one another, yet closely they complement one another, that are when culture is taken as a way of living and not as a radical. When scripture rebukes culture, it wants man, who is created in the image of God to be perfect and righteous in the eyes of God the Creator. If there seems to be, a conflict is only because Christianity is the transformer of culture. Therefore, our approach to these two should be an approach of taking them as inter related. So out task as people, should be of trying to bring them together. Christ as the transformer of culture rebukes corruption that is in culture. Sometimes without a clear cut of exactly what to follow, it is sometimes leaving people living a life of double standards, not knowing exactly what life to live, that of culture or that of Christianity. Sometimes culture is misguided because there are no set guidelines, and sometimes sin penetrates into it and defiles it, when it happens, there is need for cleansing. Sin enters into everyone regardless of who you are. It is better always to look closely, and be watchful for hidden sins.

Sometimes culturalisms dread Christianity in such a way that they want to apply a defensive mechanism. Whenever there is found one aspect of culture that might need correcting, it is better to look at both culture and Christianity. There appears to be tension in the relationship between culture and Christianity, this comes on when some aspects of culture are tainted by sin and Christianity wants to get rid of those aspects that are tainted. Even though there are some aspects that are tainted, culturalisms would like to defend culture at any cost, meaning that they want it taken on board as it is regardless of how much it is tainted. Christians have a task, since there are so many different cultures; it is for Christians to see what culture is around them without taking into account what happened in the other. Scripture guide us how to go about culture when we are not sure sometime. God inspired Scriptures, so the Holy Spirit will help us to understand. Jesus promised us the Holy Spirit, so He is always with us where ever we need help. Holy Spirit should be able to let us know that there are so many aspects of culture and Christianity that agree, that relationship must be maintained, and asking the Holy Spirit to allow the kingdom to be felt here on earth. The Holy Spirit must make us get the revelation in the scriptures. The fact that there are some different cultures make it not to be answered in a single way, Christians might answer it differently since they will be in different regions.

JESUS MODIFIES SOME ASPECTS OF CULTURE:

(Christian views on the covenant). Some of the things that were done in the old days, although different from what we can do today, they were pointing to what we are doing in Christianity. Some of what was contained in the laws of the Levites, wanted modification only because they were shadowing Christ. (2) Most of the time when Jesus was speaking, he used to say, he had not come to do away with the Law of Moses but to fulfil it. Today Christianity might be seen as killing culture, it has to be such that it is acceptable to Christianity. Jesus introduced the new covenant, although he said he did not come to change the law, but he introduced the new covenant. Those who are following Judaism are still taking the old covenant. Christians are taking the new covenant, which is a modified culture. There are some aspects of culture, which need purification before they are taken on board. It being a new covenant Christianity has played a very important role in bringing civilisation. This has resulted in it being involved in things like the running of schools and hospitals. The cultures, which are non-Christian, have benefited in things like education and health. (Warwick.ac.uk) (accessed 1.10.2020) Where culture may agree with Christianity is that used to share what they did or whatever they had they did not have much monopoly So, when we look at such things when they agree with Christianity, there is nothing to fear that Christianity will be killing culture. Christianity has always taught people to be hygienic which goes with the saying that "cleanliness is next to Godliness" this has blended very well with the prevention of the "Corona Virus " which requires to be always clean.

Is there any protocol to deal with culture?

WE CAN CONSULT THE SCRIPTURES FOR CULTURE:

(Romans 12:2) (KJV) is very clear on that without going about in circles, we know very well how the world is, and the world is corrupt, as we all know. We must try to guard against because it has so many attractive things, if it is money, we know that money is essential for our lives, but guard against being addicted, and it could be being boastful, jealousy, and lust. Let us be on the alert that we are not taken by this world, if we keep on asking the Holy Spirit to be with all our lives in order to guide us where ever we go and whatever we do so we are able to transform it. (Galatians 3:28) (KJV). Says regard one another as children of one Father; He wants us to treat each other as brothers and sisters. (1 Corinthians 9:19-23) (KJV).Christianity gives us all the freedom, but to take care that we do not abuse that freedom and end up conforming to this world. What is required for a Chris tian to have self-discipline, not waiting for someone to discipline you? (John 15) (KJV): says it all that the world is waiting out there to devour us if by any chance we go astray, let us remember that we are working for our crown which can only be achieved if we keep the rules of the game. (John 15:19) (KJV) Jesus Himself is the one who chose us when we were in the hands of the devil. He pleads with us not to conform to this world, it is for us to agree to the extended hand, even though He tries to do all that, the devil is trying by all means to take us away from the saviour, when the world fails, it hates us.

ACTS CHAPTER 15 AND 2 SAMUEL CHAPTER 6:

In the case of the Jerusalem Council, the Jews were fighting for their culture to be preserved, when Christianity was being introduced to the gentiles. This did not go very well with the apostles who knew that the gentiles had had received the Holy Spirit through grace alone. Sometimes we are unconsciously immersed in culture in such a way that it may not be realised at first glance. Sometimes there is a very thin layer between culture and Christianity that may need divine revelation to notice the difference. You cannot ask a fish what it thinks about water or neither a bird what it thinks about the atmosphere. Culture is what we have around us all the time. A good example is of driving rules, which have to be obeyed in that particular country. All the different countries in the world have their own different driving rules. Some keep right some keep left, but they want their rules obeyed in their countries. That means cultures vary from country to country, but to follow what that country requires. Christianity wants culture sifted before if it is to go along with Christianity. When Christianity is trying to be perfect, it not buying grace because grace is free. We accept culture without thinking about it; hence the problem arises when trying to bring it into Christianity wholesale.

Salvation is by grace alone through faith alone, as gentiles received the Holy Spirit without first going through the Jewish culture.

CHRISTIANITY THE PRESERVER OF CULTURE:

One thing about Christianity is that it stands out uniquely, while there are so many cultures in the world, but Christianity fits all the cultures. If looked at closely, it fits all the cultures, here and there, Christianity might be said to be killing culture, yet a closer look shows Christianity preserving culture, at the same time going along with all cultures. A Christian is happy to take some good that is in every culture, going along with every aspect that is good. It has to be taken into account that culture is a heritage; hence it would be of little value to say throw away your heritage and follow me. It would be advisable to say, how is your culture, can we do it this way? Unlike culture, Christianity is guided by Christ, who promised to send us the comforter when He was going, which means we still have His presence. This comforter guides us in all what we do so whatever we do; we are guided so that we do not go astray. Let them come along with their heritage. Man of every culture was created in the image of God, so leaving out man because they have a primitive culture, is leaving out a man who was created in the image of God. Sometimes what could make them left out could be the work of the devil who is trying to destroy the relationship that is there between God and man. The people who are fully in culture, believe that their live are controlled by the cultural spirits, to the extent that they believe that those spirits need to be appeased by the blood, yet it is clearly stated Jesus died and spilt His blood to save us from killing animals for a sacrifice. His blood was enough sacrifice. The people, who believe in culture, may go as far as to arrange an early marriage for their young girl children in order to appease those spirits.

A Christian is there to transform culture to the glory of God. If there is one aspect of culture that is tainted, that should not be taken as to have corrupted the whole culture.

HUMANITY MAY BE CONTROLLED BY CULTURE:

(Pasychologytoday.com) (accessed 27.9.2020) When considered as not working in isolation culture may be considered as shared beliefs provide a structure for our behavioural feelings and expectations. The knowledge gained from experience shows that cultural study of the mind has revealed the effect of culture on some of the way it conducts itself. The experience and the feelings derived from portraying both dissimilar or similarities in the culture of people living in particular area has played a role in their lives.

The information found with culture is that it does not have so many interpretations. The available body of facts or information indicates whether a belief or proposition is true or valid. When relating to the present or recent times the way one conducts one's self has been found unexpectedly.

Cultural transmission is the process through which cultural elements are processed. They are in the form of, positive or negative, the usefulness of something, an acceptance that something exists and behavioural written characters. They are passed onto and taught to singles and a number of people located together. In addition to its fundamental value, culture makes available important society and profitability benefits. With better acquired knowledge and free from illness becoming or greater in size capacity to endure continued subjection and chance for something to come together with something different or distinct culture improved quality or our quality of life and become or make greater overall state of being comfortable for both particular person and community. Cultures differ in in relation to the structure of the population language, non-verbal exchange of information and the importance of.

Due to these disagreements consume the way of functioning changed dramatically from one side to the other cultures.Loosely specified culture passed a matter to the possessed on common with others values, beliefs and norms of a identified number of people classed together of people. Culture therefore, capacity to have an effect on the character the way we do things we process of acquiring new knowledge, live, and act or conduct oneself in a specified way. Because of this, many a person concerned with the theoretical aspect of a subject accept that something is true that culture is an having high rank or status shaper of our personality. System of communication is learned, which mean it can be culturally passed on from one person to another or one place to another. Pre-school children take on their first method of human communication from their state of having no protection to without method words they unexpected in and out of their living places. Conversely culture is transmitted in a large part, by language, through teaching. A language identifies what group you are and also to what culture you belong. Also language will make groups to be able to identify each other. Through language cultures are able to express their beliefs, because language is part of the culture. Values can also be expressed through language. The way the words are expressed can have a bearing on the culture some of the way the words are expressed may be peculiar to certain culture. That will make a language relate to a certain culture. Cultures may differ from one another through the way they use their language. Some cultures use symbols and become their norm. The major elements of culture are symbols, language, norms, values and something made to suite that culture particularly. Language makes effective social interaction possible and influence how people conceive of concepts and objects. Major values that distinguish some countries include individualism, competition and a commitment to the work culture, learn other cultures as well that will expand your views. your views on everything, from music to food, to politics And religion, have a variety of backgrounds and experiences. Do not regret your culture for all cultures are equal you will also come to appreciate your own culture and your place in the world. Behaviours and cultures are interlinked Behaviour determines culture and vice versa. Behaviour is influenced by both personal and environmental factors, but, people through their behaviour, also influence themselves and their environment. Work and play are also determined but our culture. Others and we will make a difference when we work in harmony. It affects our values, and what we consider right or wrong. This is how society we live in influences our choices. If we work together with other culture, we will enhance all our cultures in general. Always strive to keep on shaping your culture, which will shape your society. However, our choices can also influence other as and ultimately help shape our society.

Which one is the tainted part of culture?
How is Culture transformed to the glory of God?
What are morals of culture and Christianity?
How does culture compare with Christianity?

WHAT THE BIBLE SAYS ABOUT CULTURE:

(Acts 15:1-31) (KJV) there are some dilemmas when there are some attempts by some individuals to bring culture into Christianity. There was a dilemma faced by the Jews at the council at Jerusalem. The problem we may be faced with is that there so many cultures in the world today yet there is only one Christianity. The council at Jerusalem had a task that they wanted every gentile that was converted to Christianity to follow the Jewish culture, which included circumcision, but according to the apostles, the gentiles were already receiving the Holy Spirit. The Jews thought that their moral standards could be weakened if the gentiles could become Christian without first following the Law of Moses.

SHOWING THE DIFFERENCE BETWEEN PHILOSOPHY AND CULTURE:

Philosophy helps to liberate us from the imprisonment of ignorance, superstition and narrow mindedness, while culture constitutes the raw data from this raw data is where philosophers analyse their experiments. Philosophy normally wants to move forward with the full knowledge of whatever they do this means that they analyse whatever is in front of them in order to move forward with the truth of everything. Therefore, what the philosophers believe in has been scrutinised through research. Culture is then taken as the mixture of materials with the grain unseparated from the chuff. So when culture is in front of us we have to scrutinise it so as to separate it for ourselves.

QUESTIONS:

What does Gnosticism and liberal Protestantism say about the relationship between culture and Christianity?

Christ above culture.

Going beyond the five views of Christianity and culture?

Questions continued from page 1

Is there any protocol to deal with culture?

Can we turn to scriptures for culture?

Does religion cause most of the conflicts in the world?

MORE ON FAITH AND CULTURE:

CATEGORICAL IMPERATIVES IMPAIR CHRISTIANITY IN CULTURE:

The relationship between culture and Christianity is summed up in Paul's letters, because most of them are a contrast between rules-based Judaism and freedom loving Christianity. The new thing about Jesus Christ is the cancellation of old association between God's will and particular morals:

Protestantism says, the Bible should be read widely in order to know exactly what God wants.

Culture is the social life of humanity, the environment created by human beings in the areas of" language, habits, ideas, beliefs, customs, social organisation, inherited artefacts, technical processes and values.

Yet if you have chosen to live a Christian life, you have chosen to live faithfully under the authority of Christ. A Christian may choose to live in opposition to culture: (Christ against culture) or in agreement with culture: (Christ of culture) or a combination of culture and Christianity, incorporates insights from both sides "Christ above culture". Sometimes culture and Christianity are against each other.

Christianity and culture paradox: sometimes there is conflict between God and humanity, this conflict represents Christ and culture. Grace is in

God, sin is in man: sometimes our social life requires God's grace. Grace does not give men what they deserve, but what God delights to give, in spite of their sin. In some ways traditional culture and modern culture are alike: any culture is a system of earned and shared meanings, people earn and share things.

Bubbles of legalism cannot keep sin out of the church, for example, the Pharisees were always in conflict with Jesus because they wanted to strictly adhere to the law without faith, and hence sin still prevailed and hides God's most useful tools. (2 Timothy 2:22) (KJV). To stay pure is to try to move away from things that may produce evil thoughts; these things may defile your flesh and your soul.

"(2 Timothy 2:20-26)(KJV) When God looks for someone to use He looks at the heart, so please make your heart as pure as the Lord might like to see so that He can use it. We have to be useful tools for God's purpose; we are fighting spiritual battles which we have to assess the situation, sometimes you have to move your body from things that you may not be able to fight spiritually. When teaching, whether Bible study or Sunday school, listen to questions carefully and ask for guidance to answer them. People here can have all the festivals that celebrate their culture, so long as those festivals and cultural practices do not separate them from Christ. Christ remains a rock and there is no middle ground with Him. You are either for or against Him; a conflict therefore exists in between. "Read about culture and Christianity in (Acts Chapter 15:1-31) (KJV)."

We have to bear in mind that even to this day; it is not enough to try to follow the laws without faith that is where Jesus was in conflict with the Pharisees because they were strictly following the Law of Moses. They said that unless a man is circumcised he would not enter the kingdom of God. Jesus repeatedly said He was not abolishing the Law of Moses, but only to say that a man must have faith and be pure in heart. Jesus is not killing culture, but saying let us have faith and let us be pure in our hearts. We have to think deeply and without mixing, knowing that what in the gospels is what God wants His people saved through. At the council at Jerusalem the Lord of the coming generations, He knew that they would be affected.

Whatever we do today we must think of a generation tomorrow, how they would be affected. What we have to bear in mind is that we cannot be saved by following the laws strictly, and be saved, only that we are saved by the grace alone. This is not to say that people should be involved in immoral behaviours or indulge in all sorts of impurity, but to keep away from them, and at the same time have faith knowing that grace is free. We receive prevenient grace, which means that even before we ask for it, God's grace is w we should have faith in Him who loved us before we loved Him. It is something to note that the gentiles received the Holy Spirit without being converted to Judaism or without being circumcised.

CORRUPTION AND SIN GO HAND IN HAND:

Corruption was referred to as a great sin in the Bible. Do not accept a bribe because it is a very tempting sin that many can easily be trapped. If you are in the position of authority you can easily be bribed, a bribe appears like it is not corruption. You need to draw a line between a token of appreciation and a bribe. Where corruption is not good is that whoever receives a bribe means will make a biased judgement in favour of that person who gave him a bribe that means the judgement is never fair. Corruption catches most of us because it comes as riches. Corruption is a sort of dishonesty or criminal activity undertaken by a person or organisation entrusted with a position of authority, often to acquire illicit benefits or abuse of entrusted power of one's private gain. In culture these aforesaid things have to be kept in check, the question now is how they can be kept in check. That is why when Christianity comes in to be able to keep them in check; it may be taken the other way that Christianity is killing culture.

CULTURE PLAYS A ROLE IN BRINGING PEOPLE AS THE CHILDREN OF GOD CLOSER TO THEIR FATHER:

There are so many different cultures in the world, but there is only one Christianity, that is why it is trying to unify the people, so if someone is saying let us be unified under Christianity, is not meant to kill culture, but trying to unify them under Christianity. Christianity is trying to accommodate all the cultures without inconveniencing the others Christianity is trying to influence all the cultures so they can be one without inconveniencing them. Christianity can be a key factor because it trying to unify because it tries to unify every culture. Culture helps us to understand that it is part of us, culture is a lifeblood of a vibrant society, because it part of us, something built in us unable to be separated from us. Culture influences our health, the way we respond to some illnesses, and medication may be influenced by culture, sometimes our standard of living may be influenced by culture, in culture language helps to keep the values together, culture is passed from generation to generate, it is learned by copying others. Christ is above all culture because He love every man and died on the cross for everyone and for every culture. With all our different cultures let us try to accommodate the to Christianity. Beliefs go hand in hand with what we think, we try to join them together to try to make sense, belonging to a certain religion implies belonging to a particular culture, that is why religion and culture are difficult to separate. Your dominant religion determines the sense of values. In society, we are influenced by what other people say and do. Culture is something that is shared by a group, not invented by a single person, hence although I did not invent it, it will influence my way of doing things, and my way of behaving. why should we follow our culture. One day a festival happened to be on a Sunday, the streets were almost blocked by people celebrating the festival, but in the church that day there were less than thirty people in attendance, showing where the interest of the people were most, how does culture compare with Christianity here? If we were to look at culture, let us look at a broader sense of culture, and if we were to look at every aspect of it, we would note that it is not every aspect that would be found to agree with Christianity.

CHAPTER 32

CHRISTIANITY IS ALL THE ABOUT THE SALVATION OF MAN:

(John Schwartz) According to "Transforming Lives", they would urge everyone to make Jesus the pillar of our lives, basing our faith on Him only who said to Peter that He would build His church on him. (Matthew 16:18-20) (KJV) (Ephesians 1:22-23) (KJV) (Ephesians 5:23) (KJV) (Acts 2:47) KJV) Jesus Himself is a rock before He called Peter a rock. Once we start building our faith on Jesus that means we are building it on a rock, meaning that once we build our faith on Him nothing will be able to overcome it. (Acts 20:28) (KJV) The Holy Spirit has made us overseers of that church which He Himself built, although Jesus promised to build it, we must also respond. Jesus Himself showed us how we should humble ourselves. When He prayed saying, "if it were, you would let this cup pass, but not as I wish, but let your will be done". This means we are giving Him His position as someone who has all authority and has all our lives in His hands, He who has mercy on us. Therefore, it means we are His church, so we are to put our faith in Him only, not on the church or anybody His work shows He is great. For this reason, we must be His subjects. What is required in prayer is that you are talking to the one who listens, and that you must pre-empty yourself, that means you have to surrender yourself to God through the mediator who is Jesus Christ the one who intercedes for us to God .Have confidence that He is our Father who is faithful to us. Jesus assured us if we ask the Father for anything through Him He would intercede for us. Sometimes we want to ask the Father in such a way that we are at par with Him. It does not matter what we possess or whatever is our performance or how we appear, all that is not an appeal, but only His grace and mercy. Since we said we must humble ourselves before Him, means that if we remember our sins we must confess before we start to talk to Him. When we ask for forgiveness, remember how you yourself forgive, if you do not forgive, then you have judged yourself. Let us bear in mind that He knows us better than us, what He gives us is what He finds suitable for us for that moment, which will not make us boastful or feel inferior.

Does religion cause most of the conflicts in the world?
Do Categorical imperatives impair Christianity in culture?

JESUS IS THE CANCELLATION OF THE OLD ASSOCIATION BETWEEN GOD'S WILL AND PARTICULAR MORALS:

Those who lived in the days of the Law of Moses before never wanted to change because they thought that they would not do well with the new covenant. That was the reason why they were always in disagreement with Jesus. He introduced His new covenant on the mount. He made it clear to them that He did not come to abolish them, but where the Jews had amended them to their advantage. Jesus came to accomplish the purpose of that law (Matthew 5:17-20) (KJV) Jesus was very clear that God's laws were very easy to say or to teach others how they, but very difficult to make them your life application. That dispute did not fall through, even today it is becoming easy to preach and teach others to do certain things, but difficult to apply them in our lives.

BOOKS:

CHRIST AND CULTURE REVISITED: IN THE WORLD BUT...:

REVIEW OF CHRIST AND CULTURE:

The challenge of culture to Faith, both Christianity and culture have faith but only that their faiths are different the culturalisms have faith in what they believe in, Christians' faith is the faith in the belief that Christ is alive faith In Christ can affect someone's life. Believers in Christ expect what they believe in to be superior to other beliefs. Faith believes in what you have not seen but to be satisfied that it is true. Christianity is a monotheist religion, believing that there is only one God.

HOW WE WERE THE CAPTIVITY OF SATAN AND HIS ANGELS:

Sometimes the devil comes to us through culture because the devil knows that it may be difficult to try to scrutinise culture that is the reason why Jesus came to be our guide and to show us the way. After teaching us for three years, when He was going back, He would not leave us with any direction, He promised us the Holy Spirit. Satan or the devil is only allowed temporal powers over the fallen word. That is what we should be asking for not to be led astray by him because since he has got temporal powers, when he misleads us, he will only give us temporal pleasures on earth. The happiness given by him does not last forever, but the happiness is only temporal. We are advised to seek happiness that will last. That happiness is only found in Jesus Christ, He even gave an example that whoever drinks the water that I give will not be thirst again. The devil is always busy leading us into things that will give us shame tomorrow. The tactic that he used at Jesus' temptation, he still employs that tactic today and he is able to sway many from their truth. There is no way it can be said look out for such and such a tactic, because he changes his approach. The only advice to any one is that, stay alert, keep on consulting your Holy Spirit who will fore warn us if we keep in touch with the Holy Spirit. He is our comforter, our guide and our advisor who is with us always. Let us not forget that there are some forces of darkness, which want to keep us in darkness. The powers of darkness is always fighting the light, but let us keep on striving because we know that the light will not be overcome by the power of darkness, but we have to persevere without tiring, our Lord is with us.

JESUS RANSOMED AND REDEEMED US:

It is something we are unable to do ourselves, what He did is what Christianity should be built on, to be able to spill your blood for the sake of others. We are now free from the York of Satan because He took it up for Himself to suffer for our sake. It is difficult to emulate but let us ask Him to be able to give us the courage and the will to be able to follow His footsteps. To Jesus Himself it was difficult that He had to say to His Father, if it would be possible, you would let this cup pass, but not as I wish but let thy will be done. That is how we should follow, because it is still difficult even to this day to be able to die for someone's sins, it is only possible if His will is done. The word ransom was used when the slave was to be bought back. When we were imprisoned in, the sins of Satan Jesus had to buy us back to the Father where we were unable to see Him face to face, but to stay in hiding. Jesus is saying come out from your hiding I have already paid the ransom; the price has already been paid, do not shy away, come to the fold the price has already been paid.

In a relay, they pass the button to the next competitor, now the button has been passed on to you and me, we are now in the race, whom are we going to ransom? There is no excuse but, but to act like wise, Jesus said, "look the field is ripe ready for harvesting, what are we waiting for?

Our ransom was paid but not with perishable like silver or gold that rust but by precious blood, which will not rust or lose value. We earned our salvation through the blood of Jesus that was spilt on the cross at Calvary. We had rebelled against The Father is still saying where are you, but knowing that we are naked, we are unable to come out of our hiding, not knowing that the ransom was paid. It is time for us to say, I know where my redeemer lives, and time to give all the glory to Him who died for you and me. In return for such love we have to put our faith in Him who loved us when we did not deserve it. His grace and mercy are unconditional; this should make us build strong relationship with Him.

HOW CAN MAN JOIN THE TRINITY?

The Bible can help us to understand what the trinity is and how we can apply it to our Christian life. God said "Let us make man in our image, in our likeness, and let them rule over the fish of the sea and all the dominion of the world". A difficult but fundamental concept within Christianity, the trinity is the belief that God is three separate persons but is still a single God. Oneness Pentecostals reject the trinity doctrine, reviewing it as pagan and unscriptural, and hold to Jesus' name doctrine with respect to baptisms. Oneness Pentecostal is often referred to as "Modalists" or "Sabellians" or "Jesus Only".

WHAT A MAN SHOULD DO TO EARN SALVATION:

As man had sinned through the lies of the devil, all men had come short of the glory of God and were to be condemned to hell. Jesus offered to redeem them, that are the reason why He died on the cross; it was for you and me, but the atonement is not automatic, but requires us to participate in His death and resurrection.

We have to accept and take up the new covenant whether you are Jew or Gentile; the new covenant is for all. The devil keeps on trying us, but our Lord's grace and mercy are in abundance. In religion, salvation is the serving of soul from sin which may also be called redemption or deliverance. Although we are saved by His grace and mercy, on our part, we have to have faith and be able to receive that grace and mercy.(Luke 4:18; Isiah 61:1-2) (KJV) Jesus has done what was done at the year of jubilee when all slaves were to be set free. So by His blood on the cross we are free indeed. So Jesus' mission here on earth was for the salvation of man. Man should always look at those who are less fortunate than them and try to alleviate their living standards. Jesus came here for the sinners and the poor, what we should do is to try to follow His footsteps, and do exactly as He Himself did then we will never go wrong. God's ways are in the Bible, it is not enough to say that we are obeying the Bible without putting into practice what God tells us to do. We must grow in our faith and in knowing God and also grow in knowing His ways and accepting that there is no salvation in any other. There has to a combination of having faith in His grace and mercy and also on our part we must try to live a perfect life of no blemish, practising Christianity in our day to day lives. It is not only what good works we do that can save us, for all have sinned and have come short for the glory of God, so it is through His grace and mercy that we earn salvation. When we pray, we have to humble ourselves and plead with God to pardon us from our sins. When praying, feel convicted of your sins and earnestly plead with Him to forgive you from your sins. In the very beginning, in the Garden of Eden at the fall of man, God prefigured the coming of the Messiah to save us from those sins.

CHRISTIANITY AND THE SALVATION OF MAN:

We were prisoners of sin before Christ delivered us. Christians owe it to Christ, this has made our relationship to be a strong one, as Christians we have to feel secure and live a life of thanks knowing that there is someone whose ayes are open on us day and night. God's laws were not made to make hardship to operate but to build relationship between Him and man. Since all scripture was inspired, it helps man to lead him into the truth, for a man to die in sins is now a choice because everything is there to guide man into salvation. What is only required of a man is to have faith, and His grace is not in return, because before we knew, He loved us in that He gave His only Son, and God does all what He for man to get salvation, because He wants man to get eternal life. When we sin we come short for the glory of God, the effect of sin is destructive to our souls. That is the reason why we should strive to get salvation, get, and be delivered from the killer of our soul. To have faith is to have confidence in something or trust something not seen. Grace is God's unconditional love to man, to say it is unconditional is to say, man did not do anything that would deserve salvation, but only by God's grace and His love to us, we receive it. The death of Christ on the cross-moved us closer to salvation, when Jesus said, "it is finished", He meant that all had been paid, and it is for us to come and receive without paying for it anymore. I we sin, and realise that we have sinned, let us humble ourselves and confess our sins that means we are humbling ourselves before God. Jesus intercedes between God and man, He gave us all the examples, even on how to pray, (Hebrews 11:1) (KJV) pray and faith connects us to the Spiritual Realm. Salvation is being saved from sin; a killer of our souls.

CHRISTIAN REVELATION IS IN THE BIBLE:

"All scripture was inspired by God," God did not reveal everything at once, we will have to search for the meaning. The Lord will be very much happy to reveal to us what we have to say, we are required not to add or subtract but only interpret as revealed to us by the Holy Spirit. (Det.4:2) (KJV): (Det. 12:32)(KJV) "You shall not add or subtract (KJV)" The book of Revelation was written in the form of codes. Revelation 1:10 its meaning is preserved from misuse this holds truth with other scriptures; they have to be preserved from false teaching. We have to search for the meaning. What is the intention of the book of Revelation? The Lord is revealing His kingdom to operate through man. What the Lord knows and does to us is important for our salvation. When we require this revelation we have to ask the deity for this for it cannot just come on its own. (2 Timothy 3:16-17) (KJV) states clearly that scriptures were inspired by God. We have to ask Him politely to reveal it to us. John the Elder on the Island of Patmos wrote Revelation. Near Asia Minor in 96 AD. The book of Revelation is revealing the divine mysteries of heaven. John was asked to write them because they are true. Revelation means someone was shown a vision, now it is being shown to the people. This is like what is called theology meaning to find out, we study theology in order to advance our faith. The book of Revelation has some hidden prophetic meaning. This requires divine intervention to be able to understand it, things, which are unknown and unknowable, are revealed by the Holy Spirit.

A MAN SHOULD HAVE FAITH IN ORDER TO EARN SALVATION:

(John 3:16) (KJV) says, "For God so loved the world that He gave His only begotten son that who so ever believes in Him should not perish but have everlasting life". That means before any man did anything that deserves a reward, we were rewarded with salvation which we had not worked for, or which we had not asked for. But that should not be an excuse for a man not to have faith in such graceful and merciful salvation. We received prevenient grace; hence we have to respond to it by humbling ourselves and giving all the glory to Him who deserves it. There is no amount of good works that could earn a man any salvation," for all have sinned and come short for the glory of God". The love that He showed by giving us salvation when we did not deserve it, teaches us to follow those footsteps and do the same to the less privileged. If we do the same to those around us or to our neighbours it may show that we are responding to that love by showing love to them that could be less privileged. Since there is no amount of good works that could earn us salvation, therefore, we have to surrender ourselves to Him. By giving ourselves to Him, means we are building a relationship with Him. Giving ourselves to Him means we are asking to be accepted by Him into His kingdom, where only the perfect are accepted.

THE HOLY SPIRIT GUIDES THE CHURCH AND GOD'S PEOPLE:

The Church is sustained by the Holy Spirit, God is Spirit the Father the son and the Holy Spirit are the Trinity. So when the Holy Spirit dwells in us that means we automatically join the trinity.

When the Holy Spirit indwells in us, as promised by Jesus Christ, makes us to be in union with Jesus Christ who is in union with His Father. Once filled with the Holy Spirit, we become members of the Royal Family. That Holy Spirit which was with Jesus from conception, to His ascension was poured on us.

(Ephesians 2:19-22)(KJV)speaks of spiritual heritage, means it is comparing earthly heritage and heavenly heritage. On all things of life you have a choice; you have to choose what you want to do with your life, to inherit earthly things or spiritual things. That is, do you want to live a life of your own selfish desires? Always in life you have to audit your life, that is, to always look back and see how you have been moving, where your life was pleasing, have a desire to be thirsty to do better. If your way of life has not been pleasing to the Lord, repent and start following the ways that may please your creator. By so doing you will find that you get so closer to your creator that you build a closer relationship. Build a relationship in such a way that the Lord makes his temple in your heart, your spirit will be His dwelling place. Do not expect the Lord to dwell in you at your conditions. If you build your relationship on condition of taking Jesus as a corner stone, knowing that you are building your relationship on a rock. To build good relations with Him is to earnestly seek His ways from scriptures, because according to (2 Timothy 3:16) (KJV) as those scriptures were inspired by Him, He reveals them to one who seeks them earnestly. Do not read scriptures with preconceived ideas or expectations of hearing what you want to hear. In your heart receive Jesus Christ as Lord. Humble yourself before the Lord and expect Him to use you as He prefers. Be faithful to him and He will always use you the way He likes. Jesus requires those who come wholeheartedly, He requires those who pre-empty themselves like in Matthew chapter 16:24-27, Jesus knew what would happen to His disciples after He had gone, so He wanted them to know that they were not going to suffer in vain. But, still, to be a disciple of Jesus requires a lot of sacrifices. This means you are denying all the worldly riches and its short lived happiness and focus on Jesus. That means you are taking up His cross, leaving the sinful and ungodly Lusts of the world. A Christian is made aware that all the persecutions and suffering are done in order to achieve eternal life. All this is coming as a pointer to Christians that they are following the footsteps of the Saviour who Himself went through all that. Everyone have their own cross, even Christ carried His own cross to Calvary. Following Christ is good in that although it requires a lot of perseverance to take His cross here on earth, but it is very relieving to realise that carrying His cross we are following Him into glory.

THE COMING OF THE SAVIOUR WAS PREFIGURED IN GENESIS 22:7:

In Genesis 22:7 Isaac is carrying his own wood to sacrifice him, thus prefiguring the Jesus Christ carrying His own cross to Calvary for His own sacrifice. All the calling of Abraham was a prefiguring of the coming of the Messiah. Later the Lord told Abraham to sacrifice Isaac which was a pre-figure of Christ sacrificing on the cross. This was so because Christ was also going to be sacrificed, as Moses lifted up a serpent on the tree, all who looked at the snake were healed, so was Jesus lifted up on the cross, so all who look to Jesus on the cross will be saved. This is fulfilled in (John 5:27) (KJV) it shows that Jesus has fulfilled the three prefigured in the Old Testament, so every power and dominion are given to Him. Also in John 8:40 Jesus was telling them the truth of what covenant was done between God and man. It is always advisable to first seek His revelation before we start reading the scriptures as is said in 2 Timothy 3:16, because these scriptures were there through the inspiration of God, so He is the one to reveal the hidden meaning, so if we pray before reading, He is faithful to reveal them to us. If His revelation is sought before reading, scriptures like John 1:14 will be revealed to us that the coming of the Messiah was said from the very beginning. His coming on earth was not a coincidence but planned well in advance. This shows how God loves humanity; this shows us that His love did not just come in (John 3:16) (KJV), but long ago. The word was made flesh "flesh" expresses human nature, other than divine, and spiritual nature, as in (1 Corinthians 15:40-44) (KJV). It has to be known that there are heavenly and earthly bodies as we seek to like Him, we must ask to be transformed into heavenly beings. Our deeds must always be pointing to, or strive for transformation.

CHAPTER 33

WE ARE GIVEN DIVINE REVELATION BY THE HOLY SPIRIT WHEN WE READ SCRIPTURES:

(Hebrews 13:8) (KJV) Jesus Christ is not like human leaders, Christ never changes, let us build our faith on Him for He will never let us down. He promised us the Holy Spirit who now dwells in us, if anything, let us ask in prayer for the Holy Spirit not to forsake us so that our conduct will be pleasing and acceptable in His kingdom. We may read the Bible from the first chapter to the last chapter, but without the revelation of the Holy Spirit, it will be like we are reading a novel, and it becomes a futile exercise. The Holy Spirit searches all things and all the hidden things of God.

All creation is of God, so we have to have His Holy Spirit in order to understand all creation. Wisdom is from Him, all the mercies are from Him and His love is not comparable, "Revelation through Nature", it is very interesting to note that God created man in His own image, and breathed in him His Holy Spirit, this is God's manifestation, God is ever present in us as our creator. (Acts 17:27) (KJV) He is not far from us, the good about Him is He responds if we seek Him, He is omnipotent. We seek Him and He manifests Himself in us, He revealed Himself to us through His word, we have to revere Him because He is the giver of life. God always speaks to us through His divine word. As God inspired scripture to be written, He reveals scriptures to those who search them through the Holy Spirit, the scriptures preserve for us the divine voice of God.

The Holy Spirit teaches us not to walk in flesh but to walk in the Holy Spirit if we want to be like Him, because He is Spirit, the Holy Spirit leads us and tells us about (John 1:12-14) (KJV) which says in the beginning there was a word the word was with God, the word was Jesus, the word was made flesh and dwelt among us. Holy Spirit is the only one who understands God, teaches that God is absolute truth. It is better to listen to the Holy Spirit than to listen to some misleading teachings, let us not rely on our own understanding of the salvation, without being led by the Holy Spirit, because Holy Spirit teaches what leads to eternal life. All what we are striving for in this life is to get eternal life, it has to be known that there is no other way than to follow footsteps of Him who gave an example of how life should be lived here on earth. There is nothing new, what we might be going through today, He went through it Himself. To know God and His ways and what He wants us to do, requires revelation from the Holy Spirit. Please let us not rely on man's wisdom, there is only one way to be saved, it is to obey His commandment because He is the way, the truth and the life. This means there is no salvation in any other. He wants us all to be saved, but it is us who do not want to receive, because He had to spill His blood to save us.

THE HOLY SPIRIT REVEALS TO US WHAT GOD WANTS US TO DO:

This was promised to us by Jesus Himself before ascension, even before His death, when He said, it was better that He goes in order for the Father to send the Holy Spirit who would dwell in us for all time in order to reveal to us what is of God and what is not. Since all scripture were inspired by God we cannot read and understand what is in those scriptures without the help of the Holy Spirit. So it is advisable before reading the scriptures to pray for Holy Spirit to reveal the hidden meaning of the scriptures. Otherwise our reading would be a futile exercise. Holy Spirit will make us choose what is of value in our lives and of eternal life; He will make us value things that are of eternal life. The Holy Spirit empowers us to be able to shun evil, and makes us to be acceptable when we speak, or to make us to be acceptable whatever we do whatever we do as what was promised to us in Acts chapter 1:8 when Jesus said you will receive power. Holy Spirit will make us to be able to be accommodated in the Trinity because he dwells in us and He being one of the trinity will make us to be acceptable. He will make us not to fear death because we will know that we are guaranteed eternal life. (Hebrews 9:14: 10:20) (KJV) (Hebrews 5:7-9) (KJV)

JESUS SAID: "LOVE ONE ANOTHER AS I HAVE LOVED YOU" "BE IN ME AS I AM IN MY FATHER AND YOUR FATHER":

The heavenly life is full of Holy people who love one another and they are praising the Lord day and night. (John 13:34) (KJV) Jesus was saying, "love one another" He was giving or revealing the heavenly love to us. Jesus demonstrated His love to by spilling His blood for us. That means we have to be doing the same, meaning that we have to be doing the will of God on earth as it is in heaven. That is, we have to be spiritually filled because all heavenly beings are spiritually filled. Instead of looking forward for that heavenly kingdom to eventually come, it has to be bone in mind that the heavenly kingdom already exists. Jesus demonstrated this in (Matthew 12:28) when He cast out demons, meaning that the heavenly kingdom was working on earth already. That means, if we follow Jesus in truth and in spirit, we will be able to have power over Satan and his angels. (Luke 17:20-21) (KJV) states clearly that we have to always do God's will here on earth, the kingdom of heaven has got no geographical boundaries, it is everywhere. To receive it, depends on your faith and belief. Let us observe (Matthew 6:9) (KJV) for we are asking God to make us His vessels to show on earth how life should be lived on earth through us. We are not asking Him to make it happen in the future date but now in our hearts and lives. Let us strive to ask the Lord to make us new creations. So let us be born again spiritually as in (John 3:3) (KJV) this life is invisible to none believers. The devil is at work trying to disrupt this so that it will not happen; our task is to examine ourselves so that we are not defiled, and to be ready for that life. Those who are pure in heart can only enter that kingdom. Whoever would like to be accepted in this kingdom has to repent and submit them to the will of God.

Even if there was a commandment to love one another, in the old Testament, Jesus had to say he was giving a new commandment, He went to make it clear that although there was that commandment, He had to say, as I have loved you which clarifies everything His love was a sacrificial love. That means He wants us to emulate Him and make our love sacrificial. That is the love we might be lacking, which we must always be asking for and striving to reach. When He finds that there is a will on our part, He might help us to achieve this during our lifetime.

QUESTIONS:

What does the Bible say about culture?
Daniel chapter 11: Romans 9:26) (KJV) : (Acts 15:1-31) (KJV) (Genesis 6:5) (KJV).
Walking with God: in clash with culture-----
(Galatians 3:28) (KJV) There is neither Jew nor Gentile…..

CHAPTER 34

GOD PREFIGURED THE COMING OF THE SAVIOUR

Joseph was saviour of physical Israel; again, we see that Moses was prefiguring of Messiah. Prophet Micah foretold the exact city where the Saviour would be born and described Him as God even revealed that the coming Saviour would descend from the royal, "My God my God, why have you forsaken me? The name Jesus signifies a Saviour, and was given to him by God Himself. After the first act of sin, God promised the coming of s saviour. At this very moment, Adam and Eve became aware of the fatal consequences of sin. Satan tempted them, and he is still leading people astray. John 1:29 the next day John sees Jesus coming to him and said "Behold, the lamb of God who takes away the sins of the world". Every day of the year, (world wide), Exodus 29:38 a lamb could be killed for the sins of the world, but God provided His Son to be a sacrifice once and for all. He also predicted that the young woman would have a child and call His name Emanuel, meaning God is with us.

IT WAS PREFIGURED THAT CHRIST WOULD CRUSH THE HEAD OF THE SNAKE:

(Genesis 3:15) (KJV), When the Lord said He would put enmity between the snake the seed of a woman, He meant that sin would always be there straining the relationship that is there between God and man. I will put enmity between you and the woman, and between your seed and her seed. He shall crush your head, and you shall strike his heel. At the fall of man, Jesus offered to come and redeem us. The devil tried Him at

Calvary and thought he had bruised Him, but on the third day it was the devil that was bruised. The Saviour is coming is to heal the rift that is there between God and man, as what is said in (Galatians 3:16) (KJV), that healing done by Christ is similar to the crushing of the head of the snake. Abraham was promised that his seed would be great; this meant that anyone who had faith was Abraham's seed; this divine revelation must be understood. When God spoke to Abraham, this was His revelation of the redemption plan. God's first plan of redemption in the Bible focuses upon the final thrust of Satan into the eternal hell, Revelations 20:20. An interview in the Garden of Eden between God and Adam, no one wants to accept the blame: Adam tries to shift the blame first to Eve, then to God, "The woman you gave me", similarly Eve puts the blame on the serpent. It is the biggest temptation on us to think we may sin and then shift the blame to others, yet it is prudent to keep away from sin if we find out that we have sinned, it is wise to confess our sins. (Genesis 3:12) (KJV) It is beyond any dispute that this serpent was a vehicle for Satan, my plea is that although Satan tries to deceive us, if we keep on asking our God, He is more powerful than the devil.

Paul says the serpent deceived Eve, Satan tries to all the time to deceive us into sinning like he did in those days to Adam and Eve. Through the sin of one man all have sinned and have come short of the glory of God, (Romans 5:12) (KJV), when Jesus spoke to the Pharisees, He spoke to them strongly about their lies, saying that lies come from the devil as found in (John 8:44) (KJV).

CHRISTIANITY PERFECT ELEMENTS OF CULTURE WHICH ARE NOT GODLY:

It is known that culture is something that is inborn, but sometimes culture has no faith in the Lord, so what Christianity does is that it will perfect some elements in culture that are faithless so they may have faith in the Lord. What Christianity does is to teach civilisation so as civilisation enters people some primitive behaviours in culture are left behind, so it not a matter of killing culture but perfecting it. We stay with culture, we stay with Christianity, so it is required some generous providence to make these stay together in good relationship. Sometimes man creates culture, so man has got to be careful how culture is created so that it does not conflict with Christianity. In the modern day it appears there are two elements fighting against Christianity, politics now seems to be on the side of culture all the two seem to be against Christianity. Against all odds, Christianity tries to thrive, for it is facing resistance from other religions and from culture. Christianity worked very hard to end slavery and build a civilised nation, even those who were helped by Christianity tend to forget and are not grateful.

GOD PREFIGURED THE COMING OF THE SAVIOUR:

CULTURE AND THE SALVATION OF MAN:

CHRISTIANITY AND THE SALVATION OF MAN:

There is need to define Christianity and culture, the briefly explain the salvation history of man. Salvation history can start from Adam and Eve events where they sinned against God. Operate having chosen to follow their own habits as prescribed by evil. God sums up the event as He prefigured the coming of the Saviour who would crush the head of the snake. Christ Himself brought Christianity, which perfects elements of culture, which are not Godly. As man had sinned through the lies of the devil, all men had come short for the glory of God and were to be condemned to hell. Jesus offered to redeem them, that is the reason why He died on the cross; it was for you and me, the atonement is automatic, but it requires one to participate in His death and resurrection. We have to accept and take up the new covenant whether you are Jew or gentile; the new covenant is for all. The devil keeps on trying us, but our Lord's grace and mercy are in abundance. In religion salvation is the saving of soul from sin, which may also be called redemption or deliverance. Although we are saved by His grace and mercy, on our part we have to be able to receive that grace and mercy.

REFERENCES

1) The Concise Oxford English Dictionary: seventh Edition, Revised Edition, by Catharine Soames and Angus Stevenson.
2) Talisharot; the Influential Mind.
3) The Guardian, 27 August 2017, Talisharot, Life Style.
4) Khan Academy: Christianity in the Roman Empire.
5) Machen J. G. (1993): Christianity and Culture.
6) https://explorable.com/ culture and the personality.
7) Cliff's Notes.com (2005): Sociological Terms.
8) Psychological.com (1985): Culture is shared among groups of people.
9) Jews for Jesus.org (2016): Early Christianity.
10) Mouden C. EL/onlinelibrary.wiliy/culture (2014)
11) Bible Tools.org/They had forgotten (2013).
12) Christianity Today.com/as we walk in our Christian life (1956).
13) Institute of Basic Life Principles (2016): What causes us to sin?
14) Open Bible (2010): Impure thinking causes impurity.
15) Bible hub .com/God's grace is free.
16) David Wittenberg (2017) on culture and literature.
17) Bruce Ashford (2006): Christianity and Culture.
18) Christian Re-Think (2019): Is Christianity a religion or not?
19) World on Fire.org
20) Ransomed Heart.com (2007) Our calling as Jesus' disciples.
21) Frederic E. Abbe Professor of Economics (2017): Evolution of culture.
22) Leaderu.com: Christianity and culture.
23) Paul Capon (2010): Bible Answer man.
24) Wedarchieve.national.gov.uk (2019) Tainted Aspects of Culture.
25) Wurtz E. (2005): onlinelibrary.com: Intercultural communication.
26) Bibleodyssey.org/Johannine community evade persecution.
27) Church history timeline Christianity.com/church.
28) Christianity today.com/issues: Persecution in early church.
29) Cliff's notes.com/ literature: To show that Jesus of Nazareth was Christ.
30) Thomas K Ascol (May 2019) Founders Ministries.

31) John the Elder.org/pbs elevations.
32) Davies P. E. (1945) jstor.org S M Veld (2007)
33) Chris Russel Bible Tools.org/ things that cause us to drift, Acts 17:10-11.
34) Christianity Today accessed 27.2.2020.
35) John Grehan Machen (2004) (1936) the Christian Faith in the Modern World.
36) Sage Publications (2002) accessed 23.4.2019.
37) Kymlicka W. (2018) Inclusion and accommodation in diverse societies.
38) Talbott. T. (1013) Stanford Encyclopaedia.
39) Niebuhr Richard H. : Christ and Culture.
40) Dr. Bruce Riley Ashford: Every Square Inch.
41) Christianity .org/4BC the birth of Christ.
42) Church at home.org.
43) History Central.com/100AD 60 years after the death of Christ.
44) Ma-shops.co.uk: 161-180 AD Marcus Aurelius continued the 4th Roman imperial.
45) Christianity today. Com/ Issue 27.
46) Twinkle.co.uk 205 AD The sread of the Gospel all over the world.
47) Christianity .com/guidelines for Christian living (2014).
48) BBC.CO.UK/News 3 May 2019: 260AD: The persecution being there, Christianity grew 40%.
49) Ancient.eu/Galicia: 310AD the persecution forced Christians to flee.
50) Puwforum.org/ 2011 to2019 global Christianity on size distribution: 330AD.
51) Open-door suk.org/latest news 345AD: In Eastern Syria persecution continues.
52) Impantokretos.gr/spread.
53) 53)History hit.com/August 2018
54) Edward Gibbon: Audio book.
55) History.com/religion: October 2017.
56) Role of Christianity in civilisation: Gifford lectures/book.
57) 57} Dr Sophie Lunn-Rocliffe (2011): Divinity at Cambridge.ac.uk/Directory.
58) Clauson M. A. (2015): religion facts.com.
59) OpenBible.onfo/topics/sacred (May 2014).
60) Compelling truth.org /February 2020: Human nature.
61) Spurgion.org (2016): sermons/the resurrection.
62) Bethinking.org (2015) : Jesus the way.
63) History.com (March 2020) Amp-news/why Pontius Pilate executed Jesus.
64) Britannica.com/topics/Pharisees.
65) Bible.org (2007) Series page.
66) Cliff's notes.com(1938).
67) Dr Ekstrand D. W. : The transformed soul.
68) Ancient-eu/article/the Hellenistic world.
69) Veldt S.M.: (2007) Scholarworks.org/antisemitism.

70) Rehurek J.(2005) Tms education.

71) Kinnaman David (January 2019): Good faith.

72) George Barna's Research (2011): Maximum Faith.

73) Simoneaux C P. (2015): Christian Rethink.

74) Charles Jr. H B. (2019): Bible Study Tools.com

75) Centre for Global Christianity and Mission (2019).

75a) Keel Jr. D A. (July 2010): law.upenn.edu

76) Baumard N. (2015): What happened during the axial age

76a) Braveman M. (2016): My Jewish learning.com

77) Christ's Covenant.org 9MARCH 2016) and (April 2020).

78) Cities Church.com (December 2017): Church Journal.

79) Peertchz.com (April 2017).

80) Independent.co.uk/news (April 2015).

81) Masorti Judaism (May 2016).

82) Thompson Mandaza (March2018).

83) Scobie C H H. (1973) Cambridge.org/Core.

84) Agbanusi C A. (2015): Ajol.Info/article

85) The True Church history reg.org (2020).

86) The Bible.org/series page (2004).

87) www.deakinco.com/accessed (20 September 2020).

88) Reknew.org (1 May 2015).

89) Bible.org (February 2007).

90) BBC (August 2019): Jesus healed the sick.

91) focus on the family.com (January 2014).

92) Britannica.com/Topics.

93) Chalmers M. J. (2019): Repository.upenn.edu,

94) New Encyclopedia.org/ Samaritans.

95) family life.com (2015): Culture and faith.

96) The Trumpet.com, accessed (27 May 2020).

97) Christianity Today.com (January 2020).

98) https://www.bbc.co.uk accessed (13 June 2020).

99) BBC (3 May 2919): Sri-Lange and China.

100) Desiring God.org accessed (24 August 2020).

101) Crosswalk .com accessed (7 September 2018).

102) Gospel Project .com (29 July 2013) (Genesis 1:26-28).

103) Christianity.com (30 January 2019) .

104) the Tategroup.com (8 June 2020): Forum.

105) Apolojet.wordpress.com (6 March 2012).

106) Churchtimes.co.uk (24 May 2019).

107) Economist.com (10 December 2015).

108) Blog. Faithlife.com (17 October 2015).

109) The Gospel coalition.org (25 February 2015).

110) Tifwe.org (21 June 2012).

111) Britannica.com (13 July 2012).

112) Godonthenet.com accessed (18 August 2020).

113) CSMonitor.com accessed 18 August 2018).

114) abideinchrist.com (July 2020).

115) Religionfacts.com (17 March 2015).

116) Psychologytoday.com accessed (27 September 2020).

SCRIPTURE VERSES
USED IN THE BOOK

DOES CHRISTIANITY KILL CULTURE:

Acts Chapter 19

1 Corinthians 6:9

Romans 5:17

Acts 9:26

Matthew 5:5

Eph. 2:19-22

Hebrews 9:14

Matthew 12:28

Acts 2:29:34

John 10:10

Isaiah 9

John 19:22

Rev: 1:10-11

Romans 12:2

Matthew 4:1-11

John 14:6

Luke 22:46

1 Chr. 22:9-10

John 10:7-10

Genesis 1:26

Genesis 6:5

Matthew 6:33

Ezra 10:11

Roman 8:3

Acts Chapter 2

Jude 1:7

2 Corinthians 3:18

Acts 10:1-48

Genesis 1:28

Matthew 16:24-27

Hebrews 10:20

Luke 17:20-21

1 Cor. 15

Matthew 27:39-43

Matthew 23

John 12:42

Rev.1:1-20

Eph. 3:14-15

John 1:4

John 1:14

Matthew 5:14

John 4:25-26

John 14:14

Hosea 2:23

Acts 17:15-34

Exodus 20::2-3

Romans 5:13

Luke 11:46

Ephesians 5:16

Romans 6:1

John 3:5

John 4:35

Genesis 1:31

Acts 17:27

Hebrews 5:7-9

Matthew 6:9-13

2 Timothy 3:16

Matthew 26:63-66

John 15:20

Acts 19:8

1 Peter 4:16

1 John 2:15-18

John 10:30

John 17:20

2 Samuel 7:12-16

Isaiah 44:6

Rev. 3:11

Acts 15:1-31

Galatians 3:28

1 Cor. 6:19-20

Romans 7:7

Matthew 5:17

1 John 2:15-16

Romans 6:15

John 15:8

Matthew 26:52
John 3:16
John 1:12-14
John 13:24
John 3:13
John 14:27
Romans 1:16
John 4:21
John 1:4-5
2 Kings 17:29
Genesis 3:6
John 14:9
Philippians 2
Genesis 49:10
Rev. 21: 8
Romans 12:21
Romans 9:26
Matthew 6:19-20
Exodus 20
Mark 7:7-9
John 1:17
Psalms 116:5
Exodus 29:38
Romans 5:12
Matthew 9:14
Acts 15:10-11
John 17:13-19
John 4:1-4
Romans 5:8-9
1 Peter 4:16
Colossians 1:15-17

Luke 17:21
Genesis 3:15-24
Luke 24:32
John 1:12
Galatians 3:28
2 Samuel 6
Acts 20:28
Rev. 1:10
Joel 2:13
Genesis 3:15
John 8:44
Luke 11:42
Mark 7:5-7
Matt. 28:1`8-20
John 4:5-26
Luke 4:18
Luke 6:22
Rev. 1:8
Genesis 1:28
John 17:21-23
1 Cor. 15:3-5
Romans 13:13
1 Cor. 9:19-23
Matthew 16:18-20
Hebrews 11:1
2 Timothy 2:22
Genesis 15:6
Rev. 20:20
Philippians 3:10
Mark 7:7
Isaiah 29:13

Matthew 15: 1-20
John 11:34-41
Isaiah 61:1-2
Daniel 12:4
Rev.21:6
Genesis 2:15
John 3:16
John 1:1
2 Timothy 3:16
John 15
Eph. 1:22-23
Deut. 4:2
2 Timothy 2:20-26
John 1:29
Genesis 3:12
Romans 1:16
Matt. 23:23-39
Rev. 3:15-16
Luke 9:51-56
Matthew 27:18
2 Timothy 3:12
Acts 4:12
Genesis 1:26-28
Genesis 2:17
Matthew 1:21
John1:14
Romans 12:2
Acts 15
Acts 2:47
Deut. 12:32

Printed in the United States
by Baker & Taylor Publisher Services